CONCERNING THE INNER LIFE

CONCERNING THE INNER LIFE

WITH

THE HOUSE OF THE SOUL

by

EVELYN UNDERHILL

Wipf & Stock
PUBLISHERS
Eugene, Oregon

CONCERNING THE INNER LIFE *was first published in July, 1926, and was reprinted six times.*

THE HOUSE OF THE SOUL *was first published in October, 1929, and was reprinted in 1933.*

Wipf and Stock Publishers
199 W 8th Ave, Suite 3
Eugene, OR 97401

Concerning the Inner Life with The House of the Soul
By Underhill, Evelyn
Copyright©1947 Wilkinson, R.D.
ISBN: 1-59244-808-9
Publication date 8/26/2004
Previously published by Methuen & Co. Ltd., 1947

CONCERNING THE INNER LIFE

*In Whom we know and see all things,
and by Whom we learn ever to simplify and
unify our multiplicities and occupations,
and our outward actions; by looking beyond
and through all our works, however great
and divine they may appear.*

GERLAC PETERSEN

I

WE are to consider in the course of these addresses some of the problems most intimately concerning that which is generally known as the 'inner life'; and this in their special relation to the needs of the parish priest and religious teacher. And by the term 'inner life' we shall here mean all that conditions the relation of the individual soul with God; the deepening and expansion of the spiritual sense; in fact, the heart of personal religion. I feel a great diffidence in coming before you, as an ordinary laywoman, to speak of such matters as these; since they are, after all, your peculiar and professional concern. Indeed, I only presume to do so because I care about these things very much, and have some leisure to think about them; and so venture to put at your service certain conclusions to which I have come. If many of these are already familiar to you, as they probably are, you must forgive me.

We start from the obvious fact, that as persons professionally concerned to teach and demonstrate the truths of religion, to spread the knowledge of God, and to work in souls, the problems of the personal spiritual life are of the most transcendent importance to you: indeed, that they concern you more certainly and directly than they do Christians of any other type. The very first requisite for a minister of religion is that his own inner life should be maintained in a healthy state; his own contact with God be steady and true. But just because you are ministers of religion, and therefore committed to perpetual external activities, this fostering and feeding of the inner life is often in some ways far more difficult for you, than it is for those for whom you work and whom you teach. The time which you have at your disposal for the purpose is limited; and the rest of your time is more or less fully occupied with external religious and philanthropic activities, often of a most exacting kind. There is a constant drain on your spiritual resources, which you simply must make good: while the relief and change so necessary for all of us if our spiritual lives are to remain keen, vivid, real, is often lacking in your case, going incessantly as you do and must from one form of religious activity to another.

This being so, it does become immensely important, doesn't it? for you to have a clear view of your own spiritual position and needs, a clear idea of the essentials of your situation; and to plot out the time which you have at your own disposal as well as you possibly can. The clergyman above all other men needs to learn, and raise to the level of habit, George Fox's art of 'seeing all things in the Universal Light'. Yet it very often happens that the busy and driven parish priest entirely loses sight not merely of his own spiritual position, but also of this great spiritual landscape in which he is placed; by concentrating all the while on those details of it that specially concern him. He cannot see the forest, because he is attending so faithfully to the trees. It is surely a first charge on his devotional life, to recover that sense of the forest, which gives all their meaning to the trees.

For this purpose, it seems to me, neither a hard and fast liturgic scheme, nor the most carefully planned theological reading, nor any sort of dreamy devotionalism, is going to be of use to you. The primary thing, I believe, that will be of use is a conception, as clear and rich and deep as you are able to get it, first of the Splendour of God; and next of your own souls over against that Splendour of God; and last of the sort of interior life which your election of His service demands. God—the soul—its election of Him—the three fundamental realities of religion. If these realities do not rule the mind and heart of the priest, how is it conceivable that he can do the work of God in the souls of other men?

I said: 'the sort of interior life which your election demands.' Because that will be, or should be, distinct in kind from the inner life of the average Christian. The soul of a priest—in fact, the soul of every religious worker—stands in a special relation towards God and other souls. He has spiritual problems which are special to himself. He is one of the assistant shepherds, not one of the sheep. He has got to stick it out in all weathers; to be always ready, always serving, always eager to feed and save. An unremitting, patient, fostering care, the willing endurance of exhaustion, hardship, and risk: all these things may be asked of him. He is constantly called upon to give out spiritual energy and sympathy. And he has got to maintain his own supplies, his own religious health and suppleness, in a manner adequate to that demand; so to deepen his own life, that he is capable of deepening the lives of others. In the striking phrase of St. Bernard, if he is adequately to fulfil all his obligations, he must be a reservoir and not a canal.

Now there is only one way in which it is possible for the religious teacher to do all this; and that is by enriching his sense of God. And that enrichment of the sense of God is surely the crying need of our current Christianity. A shallow religiousness, the tendency to be content with a bright ethical piety wrongly called practical Christianity, a nice, brightly-varnished this-world faith, seems to me to be one of the ruling defects of institutional religion at the present time. We are drifting towards a religion which consciously or unconsciously keeps its eye on humanity rather than on Deity—which lays all the stress on service, and hardly any of the stress on awe: and that is a type of religion, which in practice does not wear well. It does little for the soul in those awful moments when the pain and mystery of life are most deeply felt. It does not provide a place for that profound experience which Tauler called 'suffering in God'. It does not lead to sanctity: and sanctity after all is the religious goal. It does not fit those who accept it as adequate for the solemn privilege of guiding souls to God—and is not guiding souls to God the object of the pastoral life? In fact, it turns its back on the most profound gifts made by Christianity to the human race. I do not think we can deny that there is at present a definite trend in the direction of religion of this shallow social type; and it will only be checked if and in so far as the clergy are themselves real men of prayer, learning to know at first hand more and more deeply—and so more and more humbly—the ineffable realities to which they have given their lives. Therefore to become and to continue a real man of prayer, seems to me the first duty of a parish priest.

What then is a real man of prayer? He is one who deliberately wills and steadily desires that his intercourse with God and other souls shall be controlled and actuated at every point by God Himself; one who has so far developed and educated his spiritual sense, that his supernatural environment is more real and solid to him than his natural environment. A man of prayer is not necessarily a person who says a number of offices, or abounds in detailed intercessions; but he is a child of God, who is and knows himself to be in the deeps of his soul attached to God, and is wholly and entirely guided

4

by the Creative Spirit in his prayer and his work. This is not merely a bit of pious language. It is a description, as real and concrete as I can make it, of the only really apostolic life. Every Christian starts with a chance of it; but only a few develop it. The laity distinguish in a moment the clergy who have it from the clergy who have it not: there is nothing that you can do for God or for the souls of men, which exceeds in importance the achievement of that spiritual temper and attitude.

Consider. As Christians we are committed, are we not? to a belief in the priority of the supernatural world; the actual presence, and working within visible appearance, of the Creative Spirit of God. For the parishes to which you are sent you are, or should be, the main links with that supernatural world; the main channels of God's action on souls. You are those in whom the hope of a more intense spiritual life for those parishes is centred: those in whom for this purpose God has placed His trust. An abasing thought, isn't it? Even individuals among the laity who are used in such a way as that find it an overwhelming experience; and this gives some clue to the profound humility and sense of awe which their vocation must produce in priests; the constant and delicate susceptibility to the pressure of the Spirit which is required by their work.

There you are, moving through life: immersed in the world of succession and change, constantly claimed by the little serial duties and interests of your career, and yet ringed round by the solemn horizon of eternity, informed by its invisible powers. And—because you are priests—even more than is the case with other men, all that you do, feel and think as you move through this changing life, is going to affect all the other souls whom you touch, and condition their relation with that unchanging Real. Through you, they may be attracted

5

to or repelled by the spiritual life. You are held tight in that double relationship; to those changing other souls, and to that changeless God. What you are like, and what your relation to God is like; this must and will affect all those whom you visit, preach to, pray with, and to whom you give the sacraments. It will make the difference between Church services which are spiritual experiences to those attending them, and Church services which consist in the formal recitation of familiar words. We, the laity, know instantly the difference between the churches which are served with love and devotion and those which are not. And we know from this, what their ministers are like. And what you are like, is going to depend on your secret life of prayer; on the steady orientation of your souls to the Reality of God. Called upon to practise in their fullness the two great commandments, you can only hope to get the second one right, if you are completely controlled by the first. And that will depend on the quality of your secret inner life.

Now by the quality of our inner lives I do not mean something characterized by ferocious intensity and strain. I mean rather such a humble and genial devotedness as we find in the most loving of the saints. I mean the quality which makes contagious Christians; makes people *catch* the love of God from you. Because they ought not to be able to help doing this, if you have really got it: if you yourselves feel the love, joy and peace, the utter delightfulness of the consecrated life— and this to such an extent, that every formal act of worship in church is filled with the free spontaneous worship of your soul. That is what wins people above all. It raises the simplest vocal prayer, the most commonplace of hymns, the most elaborate ceremonial action, to the same level of supernatural truth. People want to

6

see and feel this in those who come to them with the credentials of religion: the joy, the delightfulness, the transfiguration of hard dull work and of suffering, which irradiate the real Christian life. You can't do more for anybody than give them that, can you? for that means real redemption here and now; the healing of all our psychic conflicts, all our worries and resistances and sense of injustice.

You are sent to a world full of tortured, twisted, over-driven souls: and sometimes nowadays you are told, that in order to help them better, you ought to study psychology—by which is usually meant morbid psychology. I do not deny that this may be very useful knowledge for the clergy, and save them from many disastrous mistakes. But all the same, I think it would be much more practical, more use to your people in the end, to spend that time and strength in deepening and increasing your own love of God: for it is only through adoration and attention that we make our personal discoveries about Him. How are you going to show these souls, who need it so dreadfully, the joy and delightfulness of God and surrender to God, unless you have it yourselves? But that means giving time, patience, effort to such a special discipline and cultivation of your attention as artists must give, if they are to enter deeply into the reality and joy of natural loveliness and impart it in their work. Do you see the great facts and splendours of religion with the eye of an artist and a lover, or with the eye of a man of business, or the eye of the man in the street? Is your sense of wonder and mystery keen and deep? Such a sense of wonder and mystery, such a living delight in God, is of course in technical language a grace. It is something added, given, to the natural man. But, like all other graces, its reception by us depends very largely on the exercise of our will and our desire, on our mental and emotional openness and plasticity. It will not be forced upon us. And we show our will and desire, keep ourselves plastic, in and through the character of our prayer. You remember Jeremy Taylor's saying: 'Prayer is only the body of the bird—desires are its wings.'

All this means that the secret prayer of the priest must have a certain contemplative colour about it: that one of its main functions must be to feed and expand his sense and desire of God. We will consider later some of the ways in which he may best achieve this. Now, let us only get this supernatural orientation firmly fixed in our minds, as the central character of a fruitful inner life. The English mystic, Walter Hilton, said that the City of Jerusalem, the city of the love of God, was built 'by the perfection of a man's work, and a little touch of contemplation'. And by contemplative prayer, I do not mean any abnormal sort of activity or experience, still less a deliberate and artificial passivity. I just mean the sort of prayer that aims at God in and for Himself and not for any of His gifts whatever, and more and more profoundly rests in Him alone: what St. Paul, that vivid realist, meant by being *rooted* and *grounded*. When I read those words, I always think of a forest tree. First of the bright and changeful tuft that shows itself to the world, and produces the immense spread of boughs and branches, the succession and abundance of leaves and fruits. Then of the vast unseen system of roots, perhaps greater than the branches in strength and extent, with their tenacious attachments, their fan-like system of delicate filaments and their power of silently absorbing food. On that profound and secret life the whole growth and stability of the tree depend. It is rooted and grounded in a hidden world.

That was the image in Paul's mind, I suppose, when

8

he talked of this as the one prayer he made for his converts and fellow workers; and said that he desired it for them so that they could 'be able to comprehend what is the breadth and length and depth and height'—a splendour of realization unachieved by theology—and be 'filled with all the fullness of God': in other words, draw their spiritual energy direct from its supernatural source. You know that St. Bernard called this the 'business of all businesses'; because it controls all the rest, and gives meaning to all the rest—perpetually renews our contact with reality. Ought not our devotional life to be such as to frame in us the habit of such recourse to God as the Ground of the soul? Should it not educate our whole mental machinery, feeling, imagination, will and thought, for this?

St. Ignatius Loyola based the whole of his great Spiritual Exercises on one fundamental truth: 'Man was created for this end—to praise, reverence and serve the Lord his God.' This sounds all right, indeed almost obvious, when one says it. It slips by, like so many religious phrases, almost unchecked. But if we stop and look at it, and especially at the chosen order of the terms which that great saint and psychologist employed, what does it mean? It means that man's first duty is adoration; and his second duty is awe; and only his third duty is service. And that for those three things and nothing else, addressed to God and no one else, you and I and all the other countless human creatures evolved upon the surface of this planet were created.

We observe then, that two of the three things for which our souls were made are matters of attitude, of relation: adoration and awe. Unless those two are right, the last of the triad, service, won't be right. Unless the whole of your priestly life is a movement of praise and adoration, unless it is instinct with awe, the work

9

which that life produces won't be much good. And if that be true, it follows that the Christian revelation, the work done by Christ in men's souls, has also as its main object the promotion of God's glory, the shining out of His Reality more and more fully through our acts: the increase of our wide-open, loving, selfless adoration, the deepening of our creaturely awe, the expanding of our consecration in service. And all this must happen in you, before you can give it to your people, mustn't it? You have to show them in your own person the literal truth of the other great Ignatian saying: 'I come from God—I belong to God—I am destined for God!'

This, then, seems the first consideration which should be before the mind of the priest, in planning his personal devotional life. It means that attention to God must be your primary religious activity, and this for the strictly practical reason that without that attention to God, all other religious activities will lose their worth; that the life of the minister of religion depends almost entirely for its value on the extent in which it is bathed in the Divine Light. This is the first term of all religious life and thought; and probably the term to which most modern Christians give least undivided attention.

Yet how necessary it is, isn't it? for you, kept perpetually on the move, incessantly distracted by the countless details of parochial life, and exposed too to the dangers of monotony and spiritual deadness that lurk in the perpetual recitation of set forms, to form early and to feed regularly the habit of recourse to the changeless Eternity which supports that life. It is the ultimate object of all those devoted, ceaseless and changeful activities of yours, to bring into the lives of those for and with whom you work, something of that changeless temper of Eternity. If you, with your special facilities and training, do not manage to do this, it is not particularly likely that anyone else will do it; and your power of doing it depends upon your possession of it. There is a beautiful prayer which is often said at the end of the Office of Compline, asking that those who are wearied by this changeful world may repose on the Eternal Changelessness. Are these mere words to us, or do they represent a vivid fact? We can almost test the healthiness of our own inner lives by the answer we give to that question. The writings of the saints and of many lesser lovers of God prove to us again and again that the sense of the Eternal as a vivid fact can become so integrated with the life of the soul, that it can reach the level of habit. In you at least it has got to reach that level of habit, if you are completely to fulfil your vocation; because that vocation consists, when we get down to fundamentals, in bringing the eternal realities of God to the souls of men, and thus participating in the continued redemptive action of Spirit on the world.

A priest is or should be an agent of the supernatural. We ordinary people hustle along; trying to get through the detailed work of each day, and respond reasonably well to its demands, opportunities, and obligations. We are obsessed by the ceaseless chain of events, and forget for the most part the mystery that surrounds us; the overplus of spiritual reality and power, far beyond anything that we are able to conceive, and yet constantly and intimately conditioning us. But you cannot afford to do that. Your supernatural status matters supremely to every soul that is in your charge; and will be the main factor in bringing other souls into your charge. And one of the chief things that will help you to develop a sense of that supernatural status, will be to keep steadily in view the great central truths of religion; training yourselves to their realization, and forming the habit of constant recourse to their healing and purifying influences.

The beginning, then, of a strong and fruitful inner life in the clergyman or religious worker, seems to me to depend on the thorough realization of these facts. It requires, not merely the acceptance but the full first-hand apprehension, of the ruling truth of the richly living spaceless and unchanging God; blazing in the spiritual sky, yet intimately present within the world of events, moulding and conditioning every phase of life. The religion of the priest, if it is to give power and convey certitude, must be from first to last a theocentric religion; and it must be fed by a devotional practice based upon that objective Power and Presence, and neither on your own subjective feelings, cravings, and needs, nor on the feelings, cravings, and needs of those among whom you work. Once you have made that utter independence and given-ness of God your point of departure, your whole onception of life will be affected; and many little fusses about the details of that life, caused by the extraordinary degree of importance we attach to our mere active service, will vanish away.

I feel more and more convinced that only a spirituality which thus puts the whole emphasis on the Reality of God, perpetually turning to Him, losing itself in Him, refusing to allow even the most pressing work or practical problems, even sin and failure, to distract from God—only this is a safe foundation for spiritual work. This alone is able to keep alive the awed, adoring sense of the mysteries among which we move, and of the tiny bit which at the best we ourselves can apprehend of them—and yet, considering that immensity and our tininess, the marvel of what we do know and feel.

A great woman of the last century, Mother Janet Stuart, was accustomed to say to her novices: 'Think glorious thoughts of God—and serve Him with a quiet mind!' And it is surely a fact that the more glorious and more spacious our thoughts of Him are, the greater the quietude and confidence with which we do our detailed work will be. Not controversial thoughts, or dry academic thoughts, or anxious worried thoughts, or narrow conventional thoughts. All these bring contraction instead of expansion to our souls; and we all know that this inner sense of contraction or expansion is an unfailing test of our spiritual state. But awed and delighted thoughts of a Reality and Holiness that is inconceivable to us, and yet that is Love. A Reality that pours itself out in and through the simplest forms and accidents, and makes itself known under the homeliest symbols; that is completely present in and with us, determining us at every moment of our lives. Such meditations as these keep our windows open towards Eternity; and preserve us from that insidious pious stuffiness which is the moth and rust of the dedicated life.

The inner life means an ever-deepening awareness of all this: the slowly growing and concrete realization of a Life and a Spirit within us immeasurably exceeding our own, and absorbing, transmuting, supernaturalizing our lives by all ways and at all times. It means the loving sense of God, as so immeasurably beyond us as to keep us in a constant attitude of humblest awe—and yet so deeply and closely with us, as to invite our clinging trust and loyal love. This, it seems to me, is what theological terms like Transcendence and Immanence can come to mean to us when re-interpreted in the life of prayer.

Surely such a personal re-interpretation is a deeply important part of your pastoral work; a part of the apostolic process of sanctifying yourselves for the sake of other souls, of making yourselves fit to attract and win other souls. For you will only bring men to the love of God in so far as you yourselves have got it; and can only help them to make sense of that world of time and events which so greatly bewilders them, in so far as you are able to bring into it the spirit of Eternity. That is what you are for. That is the spiritual food which you are charged to give to the sheep. It is that Love of God and that Peace and Presence of Eternity for which souls are now so hungry; and your power of really feeding them depends absolutely on your own secret life towards God.

Again, the world is full of jangling noises. You know that there are better melodies. But you will never transmit the heavenly music to others unless you yourselves are tuned in to it: and that, once more, means giving to it careful and undivided attention during part of each day. Do you feel sure, as you move about among your people, as you take services, administer sacraments, preach, and so forth, that you bring with you and impart to them an absolute spiritual certitude? Because if you are not doing that, you are not really doing your job, are you?

Now if you are to convey that spiritual certitude, it is plain that you must yourselves be spiritually alive. And to be spiritually alive means to be growing and changing; not to settle down among a series of systematized beliefs and duties, but to endure and go on enduring the strains, conflicts and difficulties incident to development. 'The soul,' said Baron von Hügel, 'is a Force or an Energy: and Holiness is the *growth* of that energy in love, in full Being, in creative, spiritual Personality.' One chief object of personal religion is the promoting of that growth of the soul; the wise feeding and training of it. However busy we may be, however mature and efficient we may seem, that growth, if we are real Christians, must

14

go on. Even the greatest spiritual teachers, such as St. Paul and St. Augustine, could never afford to relax the tension of their own spiritual lives; they never seem to stand still, are never afraid of conflict and change. Their souls too were growing entities, with a potential capacity for love, adoration and creative service; in other words, for holiness, the achievement of the stature of Christ. A saint is simply a human being whose soul has thus grown up to its full stature, by full and generous response to its environment, God. He has achieved a deeper bigger life than the rest of us, a more wonderful contact with the mysteries of the Universe; a life of infinite possibility, the term of which he never feels that he has reached.

That desire and willingness for growth at all costs, that sense of great unreached possibilities which await the fully-expanded human soul, is important for us all; but surely specially important for priests? It is imperative that those who are to teach religion and guide souls should steadily enlarge their conception of and capacity for God; yet how many adult Christian workers go on, as they should do, steadily expanding towards Eternity? The one thing, I suppose, which more than any other testifies to our spiritual vitality? If we do not grow thus, the origin of that defect is and can only be in the poverty of our own inner lives of prayer and mortification, keeping that spiritual vitality at low ebb. Prayer and mortification are hard words; but after all that which they involve is simply communion with God and discipline of self. They are the names of those two fundamental and inseparable activities which temper the natural resources of man to his supernatural work; and every Christian worker must have in his life the bracing and humbling influences of such continuous self-surrender and self-conquest. They involve a ceaseless gentle discipline;

but being a disciple means living a disciplined life, and it is not very likely that you will get other disciples, unless you are one first.

The saintly and simple Curé d'Ars was once asked the secret of his abnormal success in converting souls. He replied that it was done by being very indulgent to others and very hard on himself; a recipe which retains all its virtue still. And this power of being outwardly genial and inwardly austere, which is the real Christian temper, depends entirely on the use we make of the time set apart for personal religion. It is always achieved if courageously and faithfully sought; and there are no heights of love and holiness to which it cannot lead, no limits to the power which it can exercise over the souls of men.

We have the saints to show us that these things are actually possible: that one human soul can rescue and transfigure another, and can endure for it redemptive hardship and pain. We may allow that the saints are specialists; but they are specialists in a career to which all Christians are called. They have achieved, as it were, the classic status. They are the advance guard of the army; but we, after all, are marching in the main ranks. The whole army is dedicated to the same supernatural cause; and we ought to envisage it as a whole, and to remember that every one of us wears the same uniform as the saints, has access to the same privileges, is taught the same drill and fed with the same food. The difference between them and us is a difference in degree, not in kind. They possess, and we most conspicuously lack, a certain maturity and depth of soul; caused by the perfect flowering in them of self-oblivious love, joy and peace. We recognize in them a finished product, a genuine work of God. But this power and beauty of the saints is on the human side simply the result of their faithful life of prayer; and is something to which, in various degrees, every Christian worker can attain. Therefore we ought all to be a little bit like them; to have a sort of family likeness, to share the family point of view.

If we ask of the saints how they achieved spiritual effectiveness, they are only able to reply that, in so far as they did it themselves, they did it by love and prayer. A love that is very humble and homely; a prayer that is full of adoration and of confidence. Love and prayer, on their lips, are not mere nice words; they are the names of tremendous powers, able to transform in a literal sense human personality and make it more and more that which it is meant to be—the agent of the Holy Spirit in the world. Plainly then, it is essential to give time or to get time somehow for self-training in this love and this prayer, in order to develop those powers. It is true that in their essence they are 'given', but the gift is only fully made our own by a patient and generous effort of the soul. Spiritual achievement costs much, though never as much as it is worth. It means at the very least the painful development and persevering, steady exercise of a faculty that most of us have allowed to get slack. It means an inward if not an outward asceticism: a virtual if not an actual mysticism.

People talk about mysticism as if it were something quite separate from practical religion; whereas, as a matter of fact, it is the intense heart of all practical religion, and no one without some touch of it is contagious and able to win souls. What *is* mysticism? It is in its widest sense the reaching out of the soul to contact with those eternal realities which are the subject matter of religion. And the mystical life is the complete life of love and prayer which transmutes those objects of belief into living realities: love and prayer directed to God for Himself, and not for any gain for ourselves. Therefore

17

there should surely be some mystical element in the inner life of every real priest.

All our external religious activities—services, communions, formal devotions, good works—these are either the expressions or the support of this inward life of loving adherence. We must have such outward expressions and supports, because we are not pure spirits but human beings, receiving through our senses the messages of Reality. But all their beauty is from within; and the degree in which we can either exhibit or apprehend that beauty depends on our own inward state. I think that if this were more fully realized, a great deal of the hostility which is now shown to institutional religion by good and earnest people would break down. It is your part, isn't it? to show them that it is true: to transmute by your love those dead forms of which they are always complaining, and make of them the chalice of the Spirit of Life.

In one of the Apocryphal Gospels of the Infancy there is a story of how the child Jesus, picking up the clay sparrows with which the other boys were playing, threw them into the air, where they became living birds. As a legend, we may regard this as an absurdity. As a spiritual parable it is profoundly true.

II

WE have considered in a general sense the supernatural situation of the worker for God; his total and direct dependence upon spiritual resources, and the duty of self-sanctification which lies upon him, so that he may become a fit agent and tool of the Spirit. We have seen that a gradual and steady growth is demanded of him: and this growth must be in two directions—in depth, and in expansive love. He is called to an ever-deepening, more awe-struck and realistic adoration of God, which shall be the true measure of his spiritual status. He is also called to an ever-widening and more generous outflow of loving interest towards his fellow men. It was Ruysbroeck, one of the greatest of contemplatives, who declared the result of a perfected life of prayer to be 'a widespreading love to all in common'. But it is only in so far as he succeeds in achieving the deepness, that man can hope to win and maintain that expansiveness. We come therefore to the practical means by which this can be attained, and the practical aims which we should put before us.

There are features in the situation of the modern religious worker which are peculiar to our own times. The pace and pressure of life is now so great, the mass of detail supposed to be necessary to organized religion has so immensely increased, that it has created an entirely new situation. It is more difficult than ever before for the parish priest to obtain time and quiet of soul for the deepening of his own devotional life. Yet if it is true that the vocation of the clergy is first and foremost to the care of souls, and if only persons of prayer can hope to win and deal with souls in an adequate and fruitful way, then surely this problem of how to obtain time and peace for attention to the spiritual world, is primary for each of you. It is, indeed, a problem which everyone who takes religion seriously is obliged to face and to solve. Everyone must decide, according to his circumstances, how much time each day he can spare for this; and then further decide what in his position, and with due regard to his needs and nature, is the very best way of using that time. The amount of time which can be given and the way that it is used will vary between soul and soul; and the first snag to avoid is surely that of adopting a set scheme because we have read about it in a book, or because it suits somebody else.

We shall find, when we look into our own souls, or study those with whom we have to deal, that there is an immense variation among them; both in aptitude, and in method of approaching God. We shall discover that only certain devotional books and certain devotional symbols and practices truly have meaning for us; whilst others will appeal to other men. Some of us belong predominantly to the institutional, some to the ascetical and ethical, some to the mystical type; and within these great classes and types of spirituality, there is an infinite variety of temper and degree. The first thing we have to find out is the kind of practice that suits *our* souls:— yours, not someone else's, and now, at this stage of its growth. You have to find and develop the prayer that fully employs you and yet does not overstrain you; the prayer in which you are quite supple before God; the prayer that refreshes, braces and expands you, and is best able to carry you over the inevitable fluctuations of spiritual level and mood. But in thus making up your minds to use that method towards which you are most deeply and persistently attracted, and to feed your own souls on the food that you can digest, you must nevertheless retain an entire and supple willingness to give others, if desirable, a quite different diet, encourage in them another sort of practice. More than this, you must for their sakes try to learn all you can about other methods than your own. The clergy are the very last people in the world who can afford to be devotional specialists. And the way to avoid being a devotional specialist is to keep one's eye on the great objectives of prayer; never forgetting that these great objectives belong to Eternal Life, while all forms and methods without exception belong to the world of change, and only have value as expressing and improving the communion of the soul with God.

Look now at the aim which should condition your inner life. This aim, in your case, cannot and must not be that of becoming a contemplative pure and simple. It must rather be to transfuse your whole life of action and service with the spirit of contemplation. The vocation of the Christian minister is to the mixed life of prayer and service of which the classic pattern is seen in Christ: the highest, the most difficult, the most complete human life that we know. It is a life of looking and of working, which unites the will, the imagination and the heart; concentrates them on one single aim. In the recollected hours of prayer and meditation you do the looking; in the active and expansive hours you do the working. Such a régime, faithfully followed, will slowly but surely transform the personality of those pursuing it. Therefore the time that you give to private devotion must always be thought of as contributing to this: feeding and expanding your spirit, making you more and more capable of 'being to the Eternal Goodness what his own hand is to a man'—a supple and living tool. It must be such a period of concentrated attention as will gather the spiritual energy which afterwards overflows into your liturgic and pastoral work. It must form in you such an ever-deepening spiritual communion, as shall establish and feed in you an adherence to God, which you can carry right through the external tasks of your day: shall warm and illuminate your ministry whether of services or of teaching.

Especially, I think, these times of secret prayer should train the priest to live more and more intensely towards God in his conducting of liturgic prayer. You do far more for your congregations, for helping them to understand what prayer really is, and to practise it, for quickening their religious sensitiveness, by your un-self-conscious absorption in God during services, than you can hope to do by any amount of sermons, instructions, introduction of novel and attractive features, etc. These congregations are probably far too shy to come and tell you what it is that helps them most in the things that you do; but there is no doubt at all that your recollectedness, your devotional temper, will be one of the things that do help them most. For very many of them, the time that they spend with you in church is the only opportunity which they have of seeing what prayer is; and it is your great opportunity to show them what it is. It is wonderfully impressive to see a soul that really loves God, and really feels awe and delight, speaking to Him; and therefore learning to do that is surely a pastoral act? You remember what Penn said of George Fox: 'The most awful, living, reverent frame I ever felt or beheld, was his in prayer'— a tiny vivid picture of a human soul concentrated upon the supernatural world. If you are to help your people thus, you must obtain in your hours of solitude the material for such a supernaturalization of your outward religious life.

All this means that the integration of the whole life, and not any separation of devotion from action—still less a virtual opposition between them—ought to be the priest's ascetic aim; and that the time which you definitely set apart for devotion is to be regarded as contributing to something more than your own personal support and advancement. It is an essential part of your apostolic work. The gentle penetration of every circumstance of life with supernatural values is the mark of the really persuasive type of religion; and this comes neither from a multiplication of suitable services, nor from the promulgation of Christian political ideas, nor yet from the deliberate cultivation of hearty good fellowship of the clerical kind, excellent though all these things may be. It comes always and only from a very pure, child-like and continuous inner life of prayer.

Psychologists tell us that the health and balance of our mental life depend upon the due proportion in it of introversion and extroversion. Now the life of a clergyman in these days is usually and inevitably extroverted to excess. His attention is incessantly called outwards towards the multitude of details and demands; the clubs and scouts and guides, the weekly social, the monthly magazine, and the whole network of parochial administration. And the result of this, unless he is very careful, is a lack of depth, a spiritual impoverishment, and with it an insidious tendency to attribute undue importance to external details, whether of cultus or of organization; to substitute social and institutional religion for devotional religion. This tendency is now at work right through the ranks of organized Christianity; and, by depriving that organized Christianity of its due supply of supernatural energy, inevitably reduces its redemptive effect.

The remedy is to make the private religious life of all such over-busy persons aim at more introversion; and so get the psychic balance right. Their prayer should be of a meditative and recollective type, thus enabling them to give depth and inwardness to their institutional exercises : and—as their inner life matures—helping them to develop that priceless art of prompt recollection at odd times which is unequalled in its power of restoring and stabilizing our adherence to God. Such a scheme need not and should not mean any feverishly intense form of piety. But it does mean such a wise feeding of your souls as will enable you to meet all the demands made upon you without dangerous spiritual exhaustion.

St. Bonaventura in a celebrated passage divides men of prayer into three main types : first, those who attend chiefly to supplication; next, those who attend chiefly to speculation; and last, those who rise beyond both these to ecstatic communion with God. The classification is obviously based on the threefold promise of Christ, respecting the prayer that asks, the prayer that seeks, and the prayer that knocks at the door : and, like that promise, it exhibits under symbols a profound psychological and spiritual truth—namely the power and range of the soul's effective desire. It is the opinion of Bonaventura that all three types—the intercessor, the theologian, and the contemplative—taken together, are needed to form the Church's life of prayer. I think it is true to say, in a smaller degree, that something of each of these elements is needed too in every complete spiritual life : giving as they do a supernatural objective to the will, the intellect, and the heart. Some effective desire and petition, some intellectual seeking, some non-utilitarian, adoring love, are asked of every one of us; and specially of priests. The proportion of each will vary between soul and soul; but it is surely good, in forming our own

24

devotional rule, to keep this complete conception in our minds.

So much, then, for the general aim. What about the means by which we shall secure it? It seems to me that there are four main things which must have a place in any full and healthy religious life: and that a remembrance of this will help us to make our own inner lives balanced and sane. We require, first, the means of gaining and holding a right attitude; secondly, right spiritual food—real, nourishing food with a bite in it, not desiccated and pre-digested piety. '*I* am the food of the full grown,' said the voice of God to St. Augustine: 'Grow and feed on *Me*.' Thirdly, we need an education which shall help growth; training our spiritual powers to an ever greater expansion and efficiency. Fourthly, we have or ought to have some definite spiritual work, and must see that we fit ourselves to do it.

Now each of these four needs is met by a different type of prayer. The right attitude of the soul to God is secured and supported by the prayer of pure adoration. The necessary food for its growth is obtained through our spiritual reading and meditation, as well as by more direct forms of communion. Such meditation will also form an important stage in the education of the spiritual faculties; which are further trained in some degree by the use of such formal, affective, or recollective prayer as each one of us is able to employ. Finally, the work which can be done by the praying soul covers the whole field of intercession and redemptive self-oblation.

Take first then, as primary, the achievement and maintenance of a right attitude towards God; that profound and awe-struck sense of His transcendent reality, that humbly adoring relation, on which all else depends. I feel no doubt that, for all who take the spiritual life seriously—and above all for the minister of religion—this prayer of adoration exceeds all other types in educative and purifying power. It alone is able to consolidate our sense of the supernatural, to conquer our persistent self-occupation, to expand our spirits, to feed and quicken our awareness of the wonder and the delightfulness of God. There are two movements which must be plainly present in every complete spiritual life. The energy of its prayer must be directed on the one hand towards God; and on the other towards men. The first movement embraces the whole range of spiritual communion between the soul and God: in it we turn towards Divine Reality in adoration, bathing, so to speak, our souls in the Eternal Light. In the second we return, with the added peace and energy thus gained, to the natural world; there to do spiritual work for and with God for other men. Thus prayer, like the whole of man's inner life, 'swings between the unseen and the seen'. Now both these movements are of course necessary in all Christians; but the point is that the second will only be well done where the first has the central place. The deepening of the soul's unseen attachments must precede, in order that it may safeguard, the outward swing towards the world.

This means that adoration, and not intercession or petition, must be the very heart of the life of prayer. For prayer is a supernatural activity or nothing at all; and it must primarily be directed to supernatural ends. It too acknowledges the soul's basic law: it comes from God, belongs to God, is destined for God. It must begin, end, and be enclosed in the atmosphere of adoration; aiming at God for and in Himself. Our ultimate effect as transmitters of the supernal light and love directly depends on this adoring attentiveness. In such a prayer of adoring attentiveness, we open our doors wide to receive His ever-present Spirit; abasing ourselves, and acknowledging our own nothingness. Only the soul that has thus given itself to God becomes part of the mystical body through which He acts on life. Its destiny is to be the receiver and transmitter of grace.

Is not that practical work? For Christians, surely, the only practical work. But sometimes we are in such a hurry to transmit, that we forget our primary duty is to receive: and that God's self-imparting through us, will be in direct proportion to our adoring love and humble receptiveness. Only when our souls are filled to the brim, can we presume to offer spiritual gifts to other men. The remedy for that sense of impotence, that desperate spiritual exhaustion which religious workers too often know, is, I am sure, an inner life governed not by petition but by adoring prayer. When we find that the demands made upon us are seriously threatening our inward poise, when we feel symptoms of starvation and stress, we can be quite sure that it is time to call a halt; to re-establish the fundamental relation of our souls with Eternal Reality, the Home and Father of our spirits. 'Our hearts shall have *no* rest save in Thee.' It is only when our hearts are thus actually at rest in God, in peaceful and self-oblivious adoration, that we can hope to show His attractiveness to other men.

In the flood-tide of such adoring prayer, the soul is released from the strife and confusions of temporal life; it is lifted far beyond all petty controversies, petty worries and petty vanities—and none of us escape these things. It is carried into God, hidden in Him. This is the only way in which it can achieve that utter self-forgetfulness which is the basis of its peace and power; and which can never be ours as long as we make our prayer primarily a means of drawing gifts to ourselves and others from God, instead of an act of unmeasured self-giving. I am certain that we gradually and imperceptibly learn more about God by this persistent attitude of humble adoration,

than we can hope to do by any amount of mental explora-
tion. For in it our soul recaptures, if only for a moment,
the fundamental relation of the tiny created spirit with
its Eternal Source; and the time is well spent which is
spent in getting this relation and keeping it right. In
it we breathe deeply the atmosphere of Eternity; and
when we do that, humility and common sense are found
to be the same thing. We realize, and re-realize, our
tininess, our nothingness, and the greatness and steadfastness of God. And we all know how priceless such a
realization is, for those who have to face the grave spiritual
risk of presuming to teach others about Him.

Moreover, from this adoring prayer and the joyous
self-immolation that goes with it, all the other prayerful
dispositions of our souls seem, ultimately, to spring. A
deep, humble contrition, a sense of our creaturely imperfection and unworthiness, gratitude for all that is
given us, burning and increasing charity that longs to
spend itself on other souls—all these things are signs of
spiritual vitality: and spiritual vitality depends on the
loving adherence of our spirits to God. Thus it is surely
of the first importance for those who are called to exacting
lives of service, to determine that nothing shall interfere
with the development and steady daily practice of loving
and adoring prayer; a prayer full of intimacy and awe.
It alone maintains the soul's energy and peace, and
checks the temptation to leave God for His service. I
think that if you have only as little as half an hour to
give each morning to your private prayer, it is not too
much to make up your minds to spend half that time in
such adoration. For it is the central service asked by
God of human souls; and its neglect is responsible for
much lack of spiritual depth and power. Moreover, it is
more deeply refreshing, pacifying, and assuring than any
other type of prayer. 'Unlike, much unlike,' says à

Kempis, 'is the savour of the creator and the creature, of everlastingness and of time, of light uncreate and light illuminate.' But only those know this who are practised in adoring love.

You may reasonably say: This is all very well, and on general religious grounds we shall all agree about the beauty and desirability of such prayer. But how shall we train ourselves, so persistently called off and distracted by a multitude of external duties, to that· steadfastly theocentric attitude? This brings us to the consideration of the further elements necessary to the full maintenance of the devotional life—its food and its education. If we want to develop this power of communion, to correspond with the grace that invites us to it, we must nourish our souls carefully and regularly with such noble thoughts of God as we are able to assimilate; and must train our fluctuating attention and feeling to be obedient to the demands of the dedicated will. We must become, and keep, spiritually fit.

We shall of course tend to do this feeding and this training in many different ways. No one soul can hope to assimilate all that is offered to us by the richness of Reality. Thus some temperaments are most deeply drawn to adoration by a quiet dwelling upon the spaceless and changeless Presence of God; some, by looking at Christ, or by meditating in a simple way on His acts and words, as recorded in the Gospels, lose themselves in loving communion with Him. Some learn adoration best through the sacramental life. We cannot all feel all these things in their fullness; our spiritual span is not wide enough for that. Therefore we ought to practise humbly and with simplicity those forms of reflective meditation and mental prayer that help us most; and to which, in times of tranquillity, we find ourselves most steadily drawn. We grow by feeding, not by forcing; and should be content in the main to nourish ourselves on the food that we can digest, and quietly leave the other kinds for those to whom they appeal. In doing this, however, we shall be wise if we do not wholly neglect even those types of spirituality which attract us least. Thus the natural prayer of the philosophic soul, strongly drawn by the concept of Eternal and Infinite Spirit, becomes too thin, abstract and inhuman if he fails to balance this by some dwelling on the historic and revealed, some sacramental integration of spirit and of sense; the born contemplative drifts into quietism without the discipline of vocal or liturgic prayer; while Christocentric devotion loses depth and awe, unless the object of its worship is seen within the horizon of Eternity. Therefore it is well to keep in mind some sense of the rich totality out of which our little souls are being fed.

There is, however, one kind of prayer which all these differing types and levels of spirituality can use and make their own: and which is unequalled in psychological and religious effectiveness. This is the so-called 'prayer of aspirations': the frequent and attentive use of little phrases of love and worship, which help us, as it were, to keep our minds pointing the right way, and never lose their power of forming and maintaining in us an adoring temper of soul. The Psalms, the Confessions of St. Augustine, the Imitation of Christ, are full of such aspiratory prayers; which range from the most personal to the most impersonal conceptions of God, and are fitted to every mood and need. They stretch and re-stretch our spiritual muscles; and, even in the stuffiest surroundings, can make us take deep breaths of mountain air. The habit of aspiration is difficult to form, but once acquired exerts a growing influence over the soul's life. Think of St. Francis of Assisi repeating all night: 'My God and All! What art Thou? and what am I?' Is not that a perfect prayer of adoration? The humble cry of the awed and delighted creature, gazing at its Creator and Lord. ʃThink of the exclamation of the Psalmist: 'Whom have I in heaven but Thee? And what is there on earth that I desire beside Thee?' Do not all the tangles and tiresome details fall away and vanish when we dwell on such words? And do they not bring us back to the truth, that the most important thing in prayer is never what we say or ask for, but our *attitude* towards God? What it all comes to is this: that the personal religion of the priest must be theocentric. It must conform to the rule laid down by the great Bérulle: that man's true relation to God consists solely in adoration and adherence, and that these two moods or attitudes of soul cover the whole range of his inner life and must be evoked and expressed by his prayer.

The question of the proper feeding of our own devotional life must of course include the rightful use of spiritual reading. And with spiritual reading we may include formal or informal meditation upon Scripture or religious truth: the brooding consideration, the savouring—as it were the chewing of the cud—in which we digest that which we have absorbed, and apply it to our own needs. Spiritual reading is, or at least it can be, second only to prayer as a developer and support of the inner life. In it we have access to all the hoarded supernatural treasure of the race: all that it has found out about God. ☙ It should not be confined to Scripture, but should also include at least the lives and the writings of the canonized and uncanonized saints: for in religion variety of nourishment is far better than a dyspeptic or fastidious monotony of diet. If we do it properly, such reading is a truly social act. It gives to us not only information, but communion; real intercourse with the great souls of the past, who are the pride and glory of the Christian family.

31

Studying their lives and work slowly and with sympathy; reading the family history, the family letters; trying to grasp the family point of view; we gradually discover these people to be in origin though not in achievement very much like ourselves. They are people who are devoted to the same service, handicapped often by the very same difficulties; and yet whose victories and insights humble and convict us, and who can tell us more and more, as we learn to love more and more, of the relation of the soul to Reality. The Confessions of St. Augustine, the Dialogue of St. Catherine of Siena, Tauler's Sermons, Gerlac Petersen's 'Fiery Soliloquy with God', the Revelations of Julian of Norwich, the Life of St. Teresa, the little book of Brother Lawrence, the Journals of Fox, Woolman, and Wesley—the meditative, gentle, receptive reading of this sort of literature immensely enlarges our social and spiritual environment. It is one of the ways in which the communion of saints can be most directly felt by us.

We all know what a help it is to live amongst, and be intimate with, keen Christians; how much we owe in our own lives to contact with them, and how hard it is to struggle on alone in a preponderantly non-Christian atmosphere. In the saints we always have the bracing society of keen Christians. We are always in touch with the classic standard. Their personal influence still radiates, centuries after they have left the earth, reminding us of the infinite variety of ways in which the Spirit of God acts on men through men, and reminding us too of our own awful personal responsibility in this matter. The saints are the great experimental Christians, who, because of their unreserved self-dedication, have made the great discoveries about God; and, as we read their lives and works, they will impart to us just so much of these discoveries as we are able to bear. Indeed, as we grow more and more, the saints tell us more and more:

disclosing at each fresh reading secrets that we did not suspect. Their books are the work of specialists, from whom we can humbly learn more of God and of our own souls.

So the books in constant use in the priests' devotional library might include some at least among those which I have just mentioned; unequalled in their power of widening horizons, taking us away from the spiritual potato-fields in which many of us have to labour, and reminding us of the mountains and the sea. And beyond these, our reading should also extend to those expert manuals of spiritual direction in which is condensed the whole experience of deep and saintly souls— such books as the *Imitation of Christ*, Augustine Baker's *Holy Wisdom*, that wonderful old pilot-book of the interior life, or Grou's *Hidden Life of the Soul*. These books are never finished and done with. They are to be read and re-read, incorporated into the very texture of our minds; thus building up a rich and vital sense of all that is involved in the Christian spiritual life—the deep entrance into reality which it makes possible to ordinary men.

Such reading, if properly done, is really a form of prayer. Not only does it give spiritual culture and information, but, what is far more important, it also induces contrition. As we dwell more and more on the spiritual perfection and heroism which is demanded by Christianity, and so quietly and meekly achieved by the great creative servants of God; so does our sense of our own imperfection inevitably deepen. Perhaps the best approach to meditation on one of the great positive Christian virtues— Charity, Patience, Humility—is first to see that virtue in heroic action in the life of one of the saints. And it is always good to meditate on these qualities, because of that law of mental life by which we tend to become that which we behold. We grow best, in fact, not by direct and anxious conflict with our difficulties and bad qualities, but by turning to and gazing at the love, joy and peace of the saints; accepting their standard; setting our wills and desires that way. This is one of the directions in which reading of the type that I have been suggesting can be used to pave the way to the meditation or mental prayer in which we make its lessons our own.

Now meditation not only feeds, it also disciplines the mind and soul; gradually training us to steady our attention upon spiritual things, an art specially difficult to those beset by many responsibilities and duties. It helps us to conquer distractions, and forms with most of us an essential prelude to that state of profound recollection in which the soul dwells almost without effort on the things of God. It is generally and rightly regarded as one of the principal elements in an ordered devotional life. Most people, I suppose, who have taken the trouble to learn it, get their spiritual food very largely by this deliberate exercise of brooding, loving thought; entering into, dwelling on, exploring and personally applying the deeds and the words of Christ or of the Saints, or the fundamental conceptions of religion. It is needless to speak here of the various methods by which it can be learnt and practised: they are well known and often described. They resemble each other in training to spiritual ends our chief mental qualities; requiring and teaching the use of visual imagination, feeling, thought, and will.

There are people, however, who find that they simply cannot practise these formal and discursive meditations: the effort to do so merely stultifies itself. Where this inability is genuine, and not a disguised laziness, it generally co-exists with a strong attraction to a more simple and formless communion with God; that loving and generalized attention which is sometimes called 'simple regard' or 'affective prayer', and has been beautifully described as 'the prayer which articulates nothing but expresses everything: specifies nothing and includes everything'. I think those in whom this tendency is marked and persistent should yield to it, abandon their own efforts, and move with docility towards that form of communion to which they feel drawn: remembering that anything we may achieve in the world of prayer only represents our particular way of actualizing one tiny fragment of the supernatural possibilities offered to the race, and that any attempt to reduce the soul's intercourse with the Transcendent to a single system or formula is condemned in advance.

The obstinate pursuit of a special state of meditation or recollection always defeats itself: bringing into operation the law of reversed effort, and concentrating attention on the struggle to meditate instead of on its supernatural end. Yet it is not uncommon to find people forcing themselves from a mistaken sense of duty to develop or continue a devotional method which was never appropriate to their nature, or which they have now outgrown. They deliberately thwart a genuine though as yet unformed attraction to silent communion by struggling hard to perform a daily formal meditation, because they have made this a part of their rule of life; or desperately get through a routine of intercessions and vocal prayers to which they have been injudiciously bound, and which now limit the freedom of their access to God. On the other hand, persons whose natural expression is verbal, and who need the support of concrete image, make violent efforts to 'go into the silence' because some wretched little book has told them so to do. True silent prayer is full of power and beauty; but I suppose few things are more stultifying in effect than this deliberate and artificial passivity. It is not by such devices that we feed the soul; their only result must be spiritual indigestion. Once more, everyone is not nourished by the same sort of food, or invited by God to the same kind of spiritual activity: the rightful variety of Nature is paralleled in the supernatural life. The important thing is to discover what nourishes *you*, best expands and harmonizes *your* spirit, now, at the present stage of your growth.

We have thought a little about the way in which we can use our times of private devotion to confirm us in a right attitude; to nourish our souls; to enlarge our horizons, and deepen our sense of the richness and mystery of God. Now what about our education in prayer? This is a need which presses intimately on each one of us, and from which we are never completely liberated in this life. Here we come to that debatable region where religion and psychology meet. We have to use for our spiritual lives and our spiritual contacts a mental machinery that has been evolved for dealing with the problems and necessities of our bodily lives, and for setting up contacts with the physical world. And that mental machinery, as we all know, is often rebellious and hard to adjust. It is on much more intimate terms with our sensory and motor reactions than it is with our spiritual desires and beliefs. It has a tendency, produced by long habit, to respond easily to every stimulus from the outside world. It has an inherent difficulty in gathering itself together and remaining attentive to the internal world— in technical language, in being recollected. We all have to teach it and persuade it to do that: and even so, this side of its training is never completely achieved. I need not go on about this; it is a fact which every practising Christian knows too well. One great function of regular prayer consists in this training of our mental machinery for the duties asked of it in the devotional life.

It is one of the most distressing aspects of personal religion that we all waste so much of the very limited time which we are able to give to it. The waste can be classified under two main heads: distraction and dryness. No one escapes these, but it concerns us all to reduce them as much as we can. Of dryness I will speak later. As to distraction, this is of two kinds, which we might call fundamental and mechanical. Fundamental distraction is really lack of attention; and lack of attention is really lack of interest. ↲ We are seldom distracted where we are truly keen—where the treasure is, the heart is sure to be. St. Teresa's advice to her nuns, to 'get themselves some company when first they go to prayer' is one prescription for the cure of fundamental distractedness. Another, particularly suitable for those who find it impossible to forget the pressure of external cares and legitimate interests, consists in making those very cares and interests the subject-matter of the prayer, thus conquering the distraction by absorption instead of by conflict. Mechanical distraction, on the other hand, seems to be connected with the element of reverie which is present in meditation and mental prayer; and the difficulty, inherent in this type of thinking, of maintaining complete concentration. In such mechanical distraction the deeper soul remains steadfast in prayer, the will and intention do not vary; but recollection is disturbed by involuntary thoughts and images which perpetually pass across the field of consciousness. The remedy for this is a steady, patient training of the mind; the gradual formation of channels along which our devotional energies can flow.

Vocal prayer, rightly used, is particularly valuable here. Vocal prayers, as we know, give no information to God: but they do give to us that temper of mind in which we can approach Him. They are the ways in which we tune our wireless in. If anyone objects that this is tantamount to saying that vocal prayer is a self-suggestion, I reply that a very great deal of it *is* self-suggestion; and, moreover, that we ought thus to suggest to our reluctant and wandering minds such devotional ideas. It is a method which has been given to us by God. It has always been used by religious persons; and we ought not to be afraid of doing that which has always been done with profit, merely because psychology has given to it a new and ugly name. Formal prayer is a practical device, not a spiritual necessity. It makes direct suggestions to our souls; reminding us of realities which we always tend to forget. It harnesses attention to the matter in hand: captures our psychic machinery, and directs it to a spiritual end. This is not merely the impious opinion of psychology. It is also that of the great masters of prayer. 'It is not necessary,' says Grou, 'in order that we may be heard of God, that we should have recourse to formal acts, even those of a purely interior kind: and if we produce these in our prayer, it is less for Him than for ourselves, in order to maintain our attention in His presence. Our weakness often demands the help of such acts—but they are not of the essence of prayer.'

If this principle were grasped, the supposed unreal and mechanical character of regular vocal prayer, which worries some people, would cease to trouble us. Properly used, it can gradually train us to a continuous sense of the Presence of God. Especially valuable for this purpose is that practice of aspirations, or short acts, to which I have already referred. Many of these 'acts', when we dwell on their meaning, are jewels of devotion, wonderful in their claim and demand, and capable of opening up to us the great world of contemplation. They give the mind something to hold on to, quiet it, and persuade us to feel the love, penitence, or joy which they suggest.

They lull distracting thoughts and gradually train our mental life to run, more and more, in the channels they mark out. Such habits when formed—and the formation does take time—are for the busy worker an immense source of security and peace.

I would go further than this, and say that what is known as the James-Lange law, has a direct bearing on the devotional life. That is to say, that our emotions are very closely connected with, and often even evoked by, the appropriate gestures and muscular movements which have become associated with them. Thus, for instance, kneeling does tend to put us in a prayerful mood; and many other more elaborate ritual actions, which persons of common sense too easily dismiss, are psychologically justified on the same count. That instinctive psychologist, St. Ignatius, who leaves nothing to chance, gives very careful and exact directions for the bodily behaviour of those who are going through the Spiritual Exercises. Before beginning a meditation, for instance, he recommends the retreatment to stand still, a few paces from the spot where the meditation is to be made, and there to recollect himself; raising his mind to God, and considering Christ as present and attentive to that which he is about to do. Only after this pause, which is to be long enough for the recital of the Lord's Prayer, may the retreatant advance, and 'take up the attitude most suitable to the end proposed'. This may all sound very artificial; but I think that anyone who gives it a trial for a week will have to acknowledge at the end that St. Ignatius knew a good deal about how to control the human mind. We shall never become spiritual until we acknowledge the humbling fact that we are half animal still, and must suit our practices to our condition.

Finally I want to say something about a factor which is always present in every developed life of prayer: the liability to spiritual dryness and blankness, painful to all fervent Christians, but specially distressing to those whose business it is to work in souls. The times when all your interest and sense of reality evaporate; when the language of religion becomes meaningless and you are quite unable, in any real sense, to pray. Everyone is so off-colour from time to time; and it is one of the great problems of the priest and religious teacher, to know how, under these conditions, he can best serve God and other souls. Now first of all, it is possible to reduce the intensity of such desolations—to use the technical term—by wise handling of yourselves; and here prudent self-treatment is plainly your duty—the dictates of grace and common sense coincide. The condition is largely psychological. It is a fatigue state; a reaction sometimes from excessive devotional fervour, sometimes from exacting spiritual work, which has exhausted the inner reserves of the soul. It almost always follows on any period of marked spiritual progress or enlightenment. In either case, the first point is, accept the situation quietly. Don't aggravate it, don't worry, don't dwell on it, don't have contrition about it; but turn, so far as you can, to some secular interest or recreation and '*wait* till the clouds roll by'. Many a priest ends every Sunday in a state of exhaustion in which he cannot possibly say his own prayers; in which, as one of them observed, the only gift of the Spirit in which he is able to take any interest is a hot bath. That is a toll levied by his psycho-physical limitations. Effort and resistance will only make it worse.

But it is a toll that can be turned into a sacrifice. It is one of the most painful obligations of the life of the religious worker, that he is often called upon to help other souls when he is in desolation himself. He has got to put a good face on it—to listen to their raptures or their despairs—to give himself without stint in serving

—never to betray anything of his own inner state. And this is one of the most purifying of all experiences that can come to him; for it contains absolutely no food for self-satisfaction, but throws him completely back upon God. I think it is above all in work done in times of aridity and desolation that the devotional life of the priest shows its worth.

III

THE saying of St. Ignatius which we took as a text when considering the essential character of the inner life, declared that 'man was created to praise, reverence and serve the Lord his God'. Not to try to be something which he is not, or strain after that which is inaccessible to him: but here and now, with the means provided, completely to fulfil this destiny of humanity.

If we have indeed begun to do this, if the praise and the reverence of God, the awed delight in His realness, do indeed dominate our inner life, and are conditioning the development in us of a spiritual personality; then surely the result must issue in some form of spiritual service. Because man is partly spirit, and already possesses something of the creative character of spirit, his delight and his awe must be expressed in work; spiritual work accomplished by spiritual means. As his supernatural life expands, so must his supernatural effectiveness increase. This brings us to the last of the four implicits of a healthy life of prayer. It must maintain the human soul in adoration, must nourish it, and educate its faculties, and must produce creative work.

The first obvious meaning which religious persons instinctively attach to spiritual work is of course intercession. But spiritual work can—and surely, especially in priests, it should—cover a much wider range than intercession as we commonly conceive of it. We said that the healthy expansion of the spiritual life depends on the balance struck between two movements; the direction of the soul's love and energy first towards God, and then towards other men. We have dwelt specially on the characters of its initial movement towards God; the total surrender and confidence which are demanded of it, and then the feeding, deepening and stabilizing of that communion, and the education of the soul for and in it—in fact the nature and the nurture of man's supernatural life. What is the ultimate object of all this process? Surely not mere spiritual self-cultivation; a horrible idea for any soul, but especially for a minister of religion. The object can only be to make the soul more creative, more effective, more useful to God: to increase in it spiritual energy, genuine and fruitful personality. To make it, in fact, more and more capable of work: all those devoted activities, not merely of body and mind but also of the spirit, which are demanded of a shepherd of a spiritual flock. You remember how St. Teresa, one of the greatest of contemplatives, insisted that the one real object of the spiritual marriage—a term which means on her lips, not an emotional rapture, but the completely transfiguring and creative union of the soul with God—was simply the production of *work*.

There is a wonderful chapter in Ruysbroeck's *Book of the Twelve Béguines* in which he describes the life of one who has achieved this state, as 'ministering to the world without in love and in mercy; whilst inwardly abiding in simplicity, in stillness, and in utter peace'. Reading it, we remember that it was said of Ruysbroeck himself, that supreme mystic, that during the years in which he was a parish priest in Brussels, he went to and fro in the streets of the city 'with his mind perpetually lifted up into God'. He was ministering to the world without in love and mercy; whilst inwardly abiding in simplicity, stillness, and utter peace. Action, effort and tension, then, are to be the outward expression and substance of such a life of spiritual creativeness; yet all this is to hang on and be nurtured by an inward abidingness in simplicity, stillness and peace. We are called upon to carry the Eternal and Unchanging right through every detail of our changeful active life, because and by means of our daily secret recourse to and concentration upon it. Is it not in practising this lovely and costly art, gradually getting at home with it, that we more and more transmute and deify the very substance even of our temporal life? thus more and more doing the special work of the human soul, as a link between the worlds of spirit and of sense.

If we elect for such a career, join up thus with the Divine activities of the universe, almost at once we begin to find that the supernatural energy acts not only on us but through us. Our contact with other people is changed. Our spirit touches and modifies theirs, often unconsciously. We find ourselves more and more able to use, expand, and share the supernatural power received in our own prayer; and this for the most part in very simple and unpremeditated ways. This power will show itself in *you*, in your quickened sense of the needs and character of the souls that have been put into your charge; and in the conflict with evil, not merely in its expression but at its very source, to which also you are committed. All this concerns you in your vocation as priests very specially; and all this you will inevitably long to do more and more, as the life of adoration deepens in your soul. The effect of that life is bound to be the awakening of an ever more widespreading, energetic, self-giving and redeeming type of love.

Now intercession is such a love as that, acting and serving in the atmosphere of prayer; and in it we do actually reach out to, penetrate and affect other souls. That we should do this, seems to be implicit in the mysterious economy of the spiritual life. It is a feeble imitation on the part of our small, derivative and growing spirits of the way in which the Holy Spirit of God reaches out to and acts on us; moulding and guiding us, both secretly within the soul and outwardly by means of persons and events. When we think of what the greatest spiritual personality we have ever known did for us, in harmonizing us and compelling us to feel reality, and if we multiply this to the nth degree, it gives us a hint of the intensity and subtlety of the workings of the eternal and living Spirit in and through men on other men; and the volume of supernatural work which is waiting for us, when we have sufficient love, courage and humility to do it.

Such a view of the obligation laid upon us, centres on the fundamental religious truth of the Divine prevenience: of the Supernatural, of God, seeking men through natural means, and disclosed to them above all through personality. It is hence above all in trying to work thus for and with God, that the soul grows; and as the soul grows, so more and more it craves to do such work. The command to Peter, 'Feed my sheep', was just as good for Peter as it was for the sheep. The saints are our great exemplars of this dual life of adoration and intercession; that complete and balanced Christianity involving the extreme of industrious and disinterested love, which seeks to spread and incarnate in the time-world the changeless Spirit of Eternity.

Put in that way, spiritual work sounds very transcendental, and seems to demand a degree of power and of sanctity beyond the common Christian range. But St. Teresa, with her marked instinct for coming down to brass tacks, pointed out that the guarantee of that union with God in which alone such work can be done, was not to be found in any lofty or abnormal type of experience. It was to be found above all in the combination of an ever-deepening personal lowliness, an ever more vivid love of our neighbour, and an ever keener sense of the holy character of daily work—getting, so to speak, Divine perfection into our little daily jobs. These three qualities involve, first, that sense of our creaturely status, that meek, child-like dependence which is the only source of peace; next the perfect and equal charity which is the sweetener of every relation of life, and 'loves the unlovely into lovableness'; last, that unlimited devotedness, that unfastidious joy in service perfectly achieved, which transforms the whole daily routine, religious and secular, into a spiritual activity. They require of us that quiet doing of our job, in sun and in fog, which distinguishes generosity from emotion, and gives backbone to the dedicated life. Her test means that until the life of prayer flowers in this perfect integration of the outward, and the inward, it is not functioning rightly, and we are not doing the full work to which the human soul is called—we are stopping half-way.

This can only mean that the first concern of a fully Christian life is with the realm of Being; with God Himself, to whom each one in our ceaseless series of outward acts and experiences must be related. And its second concern is with the bringing of the values of that world of Being into the world of Becoming, the physical world of succession and change. That, of course, is putting the situation in a roughly philosophic way. We put it in a more religious way if we say that such a scheme of life commits us to carrying on in our own small measure the dual redemptive and illuminating work of Christ; and this by such a willing and unlimited surrender, such love, humility and diligence, as shall make us agents of the

Eternal within the world of time. All this means once more, that when in our own practice we really develop a creative inner life, we are sure to find that it involves us in a twofold activity; an activity directed both to God and to other souls.

Thus the complete life of the Christian worker is and must be, in more than a metaphorical sense, a continuous life of prayer. It requires a constant inward abiding in God's atmosphere; an unhesitating response to His successive impulsions; a steady approximation to more and more perfect union with His creative will. We can test the increase of our souls in depth, strength, and reality, by the improvement in our ability to maintain this state. Formal prayers, corporate or solitary, are merely the skeleton of this life; and are largely intended to tune us up and educate us for it. It has of course always been the Christian view, that every bit of work done towards God *can* be a prayer: and every action of life directly related to Him. The holy woman who was accustomed to boil her potatoes for the intentions of those people for whom she had not time to pray, was merely putting this principle into practice. Such a direction of desire in and through the sensible to the very heart of the supra-sensible is close to the central secret of the sacramental life. But this perfect harmony of inward and outward is the privilege of spiritual maturity; and no one will achieve it who does not make a definite place each day for the feeding and deepening of direct communion, the stretching and strengthening of the soul.

How then are *you*, in your special circumstances, going to weave together prayer and outward action into the single perfect fabric of the apostolic life? I just mention three among the many ways in which it seems to me that the clergy can do this: making their inner life of prayer continuously and directly useful to those to

47

whom they are sent, incorporating it with their pastoral activities.

I put first a very simple thing; a thing which I imagine that almost everyone can do, and which I have never known to fail in its effect. It is this. Make time to pray in your own churches as much as you possibly can. That is the first move towards making these churches real houses, schools, and homes of prayer, which very often they are not. I do not mean by this merely saying Matins and Evensong in them. I mean, let at least part of the time which is given to your real and informal communion with God be spent in your own church. That is the best and most certain way in which to give our churches the atmosphere of devotion which we all recognize so quickly when we find it, and which turns them into spiritual homes; and I believe it is one of the most valuable forms of Christian witness which can be exercised by the clergy in the present day.

It seems to me that it is very little use to keep a church open, unless its own priest does care to go into it and pray in it. You might just as well, in most cases, keep a waiting room open. Surely it is part of your business to make your church homely and lovable, and especially, if you can, to give it a welcoming aspect at those hours when the working people who so greatly need its tranquillizing atmosphere can inconspicuously slip in. It is useless to talk at large to those working people, mostly living without privacy in noisy streets, about the reality and necessity of prayer unless you provide a quiet place in which they can practise it. It must be a place which does not receive them with that forbidding air of a spiritual drawing-room in dust sheets, peculiar to many Anglican churches during the week; but which abounds in suitable suggestions, offers an invitation which it helps them to accept. A place in fact, to which your own prayers have helped to give the requisite quality of homeliness. This creation of a real supernatural home, and steady practice of a real supernatural hospitality, is the first point, it seems to me, in which a clergyman can hardly fail to make his inner life directly serve his flock.

The next direction in which it is possible for you to make your self-training in prayer useful to those in your charge falls under the general head of intercession. That will of course include all that you can do for your parish and for individuals in the way of support, in the way of tranquillizing and healing influences, in the way of supernatural guidance, by the loving meditations and prayers which you spend upon them. Those who deal much with souls soon come to know something about the strange spiritual currents which are at work under the surface of life, and the extent in which charity can work on supernatural levels for supernatural ends. But if you are to do that, the one thing that matters is that you should care supremely about it; care, in fact, so much that you do not mind how much you suffer for it. We cannot help anyone until we do care, for it is only by love that spirit penetrates spirit.

Consider for a moment what is implied in this amazing mystery of intercession; at least in the little that we understand of it. It implies first our implicit realization of God, the infinitely loving, living and all-penetrating Spirit of Spirits, as an Ocean in which we all are bathed. And next, speaking still that spatial language to which our human thinking is tied down, that somehow through this uniting and vivifying medium we too, being one with Him in love and will, can mutually penetrate, move and influence each other's souls in ways as yet unguessed; yet throughout the whole process moulded and determined by the prevenient, personal, free and ever-present God. The world He has been and is creating is a world infused

49

through and through with Spirit; and it is partly through the prayerful and God-inspired action of men that the spiritual work of this world is done. When a man or woman of prayer, through their devoted concentration, reaches a soul in temptation and rescues it, we must surely acknowledge that this is the action of God Himself, using that person as an instrument.

In this mysterious interaction of energies it seems that one tool is put into our hands: our love, will, interest, desire—four words describing four aspects of one thing. This dynamic love, once purged of self-interest, is ours to use on spiritual levels; it is an engine for working with God on other souls. The saints so used it, often at tremendous cost to themselves, and with tremendous effect. As their personality grew in strength and expanded in adoration, so they were drawn on to desperate and heroic wrestling for souls; to those exhausting and creative activities, that steady and generous giving of support, that redeeming prayer by which human spirits are called to work with God. Especially in its most mysterious reaches, in its redemptive, self-immolating action on suffering and sin, their intercession dimly reproduces and continues the supernatural work of Christ. Real saints do feel and bear the weight of the sins and pains of the world. It is the human soul's greatest privilege that we can thus accept redemptive suffering for one another—and they do.

'God *enabled* me to agonize in prayer,' said the saintly Evangelical, David Brainerd. 'My soul was drawn out very much for the world. I grasped for a multitude of souls.' Does not that give to us a sense of unreached possibilities, of deep mysterious energies; something not quite covered by what are usually called 'intercessions'? So too St. Teresa says that if anyone claiming to be united to God is always in a state of peaceful beatitude, she simply does not believe in their union with God. Such a union, to her mind, involves great sorrow for the sin and pain of the world; a sense of identity not only with God but also with all other souls, and a great longing to redeem and heal. ⁺ That is real supernatural charity. ⁺ It is a call to love and save not the nice but the nasty; not the lovable but the unlovely, the hard, the narrow, and the embittered, and the tiresome, who are so much worse. To love irrespective of merit or opinion or personal preference; to love even those who offend our taste. If you are to love your people thus, translating your love, as you must, into unremitting intercessory work, and avoid being swamped by the great ocean of suffering, sin and need to which you are sent; once again this will only be done by maintaining and feeding the temper of adoration and trustful adherence. This is the heart of the life of prayer; and only in so far as we work from this centre can we safely dare to touch other souls and seek to affect them. For such intercession is a sacrificial job; and sacrificial jobs need the support of a strong inner life if they are to be carried through. They are rooted and grounded in love.

The third obvious way in which the priest's life of prayer reacts upon his flock, is in the personal advice and guidance which he is able to give to those who consult him—to use a technical word, in direction work. What is direction? It is the guidance of one soul by and through another soul. It is the individual and intensive side of pastoral work. God comes to and affects individuals very largely through other individuals; and you, in your ordination, all offered yourselves for this. The relation of discipleship is one that obtains right through and down all stages of the spiritual life; giving to it a definite social structure, protecting it from subjectivism and lawlessness and ensuring its continuity. Hence all that we may have been given or gained we ought ever to be ready to impart.

Such direction work is surely one of the most sacred of human duties; and as your inner life becomes stronger and your spiritual sensitiveness increases, so more souls will inevitably come to you for it, and more and more of its difficulties and possibilities will be revealed. Therefore a solemn obligation rests on the priest, doesn't it? to train his mind as well as his soul for this work; to learn, for instance, something of the mental peculiarities of man, especially as they affect his religious life; to recognize the various stages and types of spirituality, and find out how best to deal with them; to discern spirits, and to distinguish their different aptitudes and needs. In its fullness such discernment is a special gift; but something of it is surely possible to all of us, if we take enough interest in souls. Direction work can of course be done only and all the time in absolute interior dependence on God; and all the most valuable part of it will be done silently, by the influence of your prayer on the souls that you are called upon to guide. You will find it a perfectly possible and practicable thing to reach out to them and mould them in that way; and if they are at all sensitive, they will probably become aware that you are doing it.

Amongst those who are likely to come to a clergyman for spiritual advice are three outstanding classes. First, quite young people, including Confirmation candidates, who are at the beginning of their spiritual, mental and emotional lives, and wish for guidance in religion. Secondly, adults who have lost their faith, or have never had it, but who now want to be helped to find God. Thirdly, adults who are still Christian, but who are tortured by doubts, or over-tried by life; and who want to be helped not to lose God. Here the first principle surely is that in each class each person must be envisaged separately; and in each case the directing soul must think first not of its own point of view, not of any set doctrinal scheme, any 'Catholic' or 'Evangelical' principles, but of that one inquiring soul in its special needs, its special stage of advancement, its special relation to God.

You are face to face with a living, growing, individual spirit; not a lump of wax on which to stamp the Christian seal. And you are responsible to God, not for giving that soul a bit of orthodox information, which it probably won't understand: but for helping it to see its own whereabouts, actualize in its own way its particular spiritual capacities, that it may gradually become more real, and fulfil its latent genius for sanctity. Hence the first temptation which the director must conquer at all costs, is the inclination to generalize, to apply stock ideas. Even with the young and untried, routine instructions and methods are often dangerous; for already, at the very beginning, soul differs immensely from soul. A great respect for every type and size, homely patience, humble self-oblivion, a sense of the slowness of real spiritual growth; these are the qualities which make the good director. The teacher is often inclined to force the pace with the ardent; whereas wise moderation in direction, a gentle willingness to wait, is perhaps the one thing that is always safe with everyone all the time.

With the second and third class of souls it is of course even more imperative to be self-oblivious, slow and tentative; for here you are dealing with more or less developed but troubled minds, alertly awake to the least hint of unreality, suspicious of theological formulas, and probably unwilling to accept without criticism anything that you say. Moreover, you are necessarily only partly acquainted with their mental furnishing and outlook; and therefore it is never possible for you to be certain what exact meaning your words will convey, and what effect they will produce. The emotional aura surrounding religious ideas is of all things most difficult to estimate. Your pet symbols may turn out to be those which are most calculated to put your pupils off. In dealing with such cases, you are or should be perpetually thrown back on God. You can only hope to deal with them at all in a spirit of prayer; and in constant remembrance that the one thing which really matters is the contagious character of your own certitude, never the argument by which it is expressed. So done, the result of your work will often surprise you, and seem to bear little relation to anything that you have been able to say.

Even with those persons who are or seem most impressionable and most sympathetic to you, it is a help to realize from the first that you will never be able to make another soul see reality from exactly the same spiritual angle as yourself. You will not, indeed, be able to transfer even the most fundamental of your convictions to them with no change of colour or meaning. Nor should you wish to do so; for a good deal of that colour and emphasis is your personal contribution, and has little to do with absolute truth. Your pupils inevitably bring to their encounter with God a psychic content which is entirely different from yours; hence, in psychological language, their apperceptive mass will be peculiar to themselves, coloured by their education, tastes, character, past history, and social environment. Now apperception controls all our religious insights and experiences; which, so long as we are in the body, cannot by any possibility be pure. The result of this psychological law is that your most careful and precise teaching often fails to find acceptance; or else comes back to you in an unrecognizable form. This, if you attribute absolute value to the particular terms in which you gave it, may be a very

54

disheartening experience, and administer a sound slap to professional self-esteem.

But in proportion as your interior life of prayer grows deep, tender and selfless, in proportion as you value forms only as the clothing of inwardly perceived realities, so will you be able to get away from the conventional phraseology which now puts many people off so terribly, and adapt your language to the particular circumstances of each soul. It is a remarkable note of the Gospels that they make clear to us how many different ways our Lord had of saying the same thing; how He met each type on its own ground, and was satisfied to ask some to find the Father through contemplation of the lilies, whilst of others was demanded self-stripping and the Cross. And it still remains true that the most saintly teachers are always the most varied, winning, unrigoristic, and persuasive in their methods; however hard and costly the demands which they may ultimately make.

This means seeing all such work from a really pastoral angle; keeping your eye steadily on the size, sort, appetite, and future development of each particular sheep, trying to help each to achieve *their* sort of perfection, not yours, refusing the temptation to 'form a type', and aiming all the time at life, more abundant life for each, and the giving and fostering of it. Not at imparting information, but providing suitable food which can and must be digested; and changed, as real food must be in the process, in order that it may nourish the life of the creature fed. When you see the situation in this way, you cease to mind the fact that those bits which *you* think the very best are often ignored, and your most careful suggestions and instructions are apparently misunderstood. After all, the spiritual personality you are helping to form, is probably quite different from your own; and perhaps even different from your own secret ideal for it. Hence the very things that may seem to you most essential or most excellent must not always be pressed. Mangel-wurzels do not suit every sheep at every stage of its growth. It needs a great deal of self-abandonment to do all this with simplicity—it means learning from those who come to you, as well as trying to teach—and that is the purifying part of personal religious work.

Moreover, those who do this work are commonly themselves growing and changing; they have not arrived, but are travelling and exploring as they go. It is generally a case of one more or less dusty pilgrim helping another *in via*; not of an established professor, who knows all about it, administering stock teaching to a docile student. It may very well happen that someone will come to you for advice, who has had or seems to have had spiritual experiences far beyond your present range; or who had been called to a form of prayer of which you know nothing at first hand. What is to be done about that? How are you going to distinguish the victims of nervous illness or of religious vanity from those who have a genuine drawing to religion of the mystical type? And how, in this latter case—the case of those drawn by God to the mystical degrees of prayer, often to their own great bewilderment—are you going to give just the help and guidance their souls need, in regions where you yourself have never been? This humbling duty may be laid at any moment on any clergyman; and it will be an awful thing, won't it? if you have concentrated so entirely on the parochial, ethical and humanitarian side of religion that you have nothing to give souls that are called to practise its deeper mysteries.

This is where a strict personal training in mental prayer and spiritual reading abundantly justifies itself. You may not yourself be called to the mountains; but you will be more able to advise and understand prospective mountaineers if you have at least put on heavy boots and tried a little hill climbing, than if you have merely spent all your time on the level, growing nice little patches of devotional mustard and cress. And those who thus form and maintain in themselves the disciplined habit of attention to God, who exercise their spiritual muscles, quicken their spiritual senses, and try to learn their business from the saints, do develop the power of discriminating the self-deluded from the genuine mystical type; by no means an easy thing to do. They recognize the real thing when they meet it; and have access to sources of information which they know how to apply, and which do enable them to help it. There is no doubt at all that human souls can be and are thus used by God, to help other souls more spiritually advanced than themselves; but only if they are in touch through surrendered prayer with the sources of spiritual light. It is useless, indeed dangerous, to read works on mystical prayer and presume to apply them, unless we have to some extent sought to practise the discipline of recollection ourselves. We think that we understand them, and we don't; we try to apply them, and come hopelessly to grief. Spiritual books are written in the language of the spirit; and must be spiritually discerned. They yield a new sense at every reading; and it is only after many years that most of us begin to realize the colossal nature of our own initial mistakes. Hence it is imperative that those called to guide the souls of others, should themselves be humble pupils in the school of interior prayer.

This idea of the call of God to one soul to be the director, support, and light-giver to another soul, has rather fallen out of our English religious life. It is at present only practised in one branch of the Church; and there very often in what seems to be an unnecessarily hot-housey way. The detailed and personal work in souls done in past ages by the numerous men and women, both lay and religious, who transmitted the science of the spiritual life, is now forgotten. We are much concerned about various kinds of education; but we leave wholly on one side this parental, patient and expert training and cherishing of the spirit. And yet how beautiful, how Christian, and how natural an idea it is! The work of the great French directors—Fénelon, Boussuet, François de Sa'es, Vincent de Paul—shows what it can do, and what gentle wisdom, moderation, flexibility, psychological insight, selfless patience, and spiritual firmness it demands. Their letters of direction, which ought surely to be read and re-read by every priest, are full of that sanctified common sense which weaves together with a firm hand the worlds of nature and of grace; and helps the pupil soul to find, in all the ordinary circumstances of life, material for prayer and discipline and an opportunity of getting nearer to reality. I think the revival, in a form adapted to our times, of such personal direction work would do much to renew the life of prayer within the English Church; and it cannot be restored without a sufficiency of clergy able to undertake it. Those who are able are not likely to lack pupils very long: they are easily recognized, and the present widespread hunger for the things of the spirit does the rest.

Now let us sum up the substance of what we have been considering. First, the obvious truth that the servant of God cannot do his best unless he is his best: and therefore self-deepening and self-improvement are the very heart of his job. Secondly, that being one's best, for Christians, depends on and requires the active co-operation and close union of God's grace and man's will: docility and effort both at once. That this union of serene docility and costly effort, then, must rule in the priest's life of prayer: for the object of that life of prayer is the deepening and expanding of his own inner life, an ever more perfect self-oblation, in order that he may be able to apprehend, receive, and pass on to others more and more of the abundant secrets of Eternal Life. Out of *your* struggles and temptations, *your* tentative glimpses of reality, *your* generous acts of utter self-abandonment to the purposes of God—out of all these different kinds of purification taken together, something has to be made, with which the Holy Spirit can do His work on other souls. Because that is the way in which He does do His work on other souls.

In other words: Our deepest life consists in a willed correspondence with the world of Spirit, and this willed correspondence, which is prayer, is destined to fulfil itself along two main channels; in love towards God and in love towards humanity—two loves which at last and at their highest become one love. Sooner or later, in varying degrees, the power and redeeming energy of God will be manifested through those who thus reach out in desire, first towards Him and then towards other souls. And we, living and growing personalities, are required to become ever more and more spiritualized, ever more and more persuasive, more and more deeply real; in order that we may fulfil this Divine purpose.

This is not mere pious fluff. This is a terribly practical job; the only way in which we can contribute to the bringing in of the Kingdom of God. Humanitarian politics will not do it. Theological restatement will not do it. Holiness *will* do it. And for this growth towards holiness, it seems that it is needful to practise, and practise together, both that genuine peaceful recollection in which the soul tastes, and really knows that the Lord is sweet, inwardly abiding in His stillness and peace; and also the suffering, effort and tension required of us unstable human creatures, if we are to maintain that interior state and use it for the good of other men. This ideal is so rich, that in its wholeness it has only been satisfied once. Yet it is so elastic, that within it every faithful personality can find a place and opportunity of development. It means the practice of both attachment and detachment; the most careful and loving fulfilment of all our varied this-world obligations, without any slackening of attachment to the other-worldly love.

And if we want a theoretical justification of such a scheme of life, surely we have it in the central Christian doctrine of the Incarnation? For does not this mean the Eternal, Changeless God reaching out to win and eternalize His creatures by contact through personality? that the direct action of Divine Love on man is through man; and that God requires our growth in personality, in full being, in order that through us His love and holiness can more and more fully be expressed? And our Lord's life of ministry supported by much lonely prayer gives us the classic pattern of human correspondence with this, our two-fold environment. The saints tried to imitate that pattern more and more closely; and as they did so, their personality expanded and shone with love and power. They show us in history a growth and transformation of character which we are not able to grasp; yet which surely ought to be the Christian norm? In many cases they were such ordinary, even unpromising people when they began; for the real saint is neither a special creation nor a spiritual freak. He is just a human being in whom has been fulfilled the great aspiration of St. Augustine—'My life shall be a real life, being wholly full of Thee.' And as that real life, that interior union with God grows, so too does the saints' self-identification with humanity grow. They do not stand aside wrapped in delightful prayers and feeling pure and agreeable to God. They go right down into the mess; and there, right down in the mess, they are able to radiate God because they possess Him. And that, above all else, is the priestly work that wins and heals souls.

THE HOUSE OF THE SOUL

However great the breadth, the depth, the height of our thought of the soul, we shall not exceed the reality; for its capacity is far greater than we are able to conceive, and the Sun which dwells in this house penetrates to every corner of it.

ST. TERESA

FOR ROSA

WITH MY LOVE

I

WHEN St. Paul described our mysterious human nature as a 'Temple of the Holy Spirit'—a created dwelling-place or sanctuary of the uncreated and invisible Divine Life—he was stating in the strongest possible terms a view of our status, our relation to God, which has always been present in Christianity; and is indeed implicit in the Christian view of Reality. But that statement as it stands seems far too strong for most of us. We do not feel in the very least like the temples of Creative Love. We are more at ease with St. Teresa, when she describes the soul as an 'interior castle'—a roomy mansion, with various floors and apartments from the basement upwards; not all devoted to exalted uses, not always in a satisfactory state. And when, in a more homely mood, she speaks of her own spiritual life as 'becoming solid like a house', we at last get something we can grasp.

The soul's house, that interior dwelling-place which we all possess, for the upkeep of which we are responsible —a place in which we can meet God, or from which in a sense we can exclude God—that is not too big an idea for us. Though no imagery drawn from the life of sense can ever be adequate to the strange and delicate contacts, tensions, demands and benedictions of the life that lies beyond sense: though the important part of every parable is that which it fails to express: still, here is a conception which can be made to cover many of the truths that govern the interior life of prayer.

First, we are led to consider the position of the house. However interesting and important its peculiarities may seem to the tenant, it is not as a matter of fact an unusually picturesque and interesting mansion made to an original design, and set in its own grounds with no other building in sight. Christian spirituality knows nothing of this sort of individualism. It insists that we do not inhabit detached residences, but are parts of a vast spiritual organism; that even the most hidden life is never lived for itself alone. Our soul's house forms part of the vast City of God. Though it may not be an important mansion with a frontage on the main street, nevertheless it shares all the obligations and advantages belonging to the city as a whole. It gets its water from the main, and its light from the general supply. The way we maintain and use it must have reference to our civic responsibilities.

It is true that God creates souls in a marvellous liberty and variety. The ideals of the building-estate tell us nothing about the Kingdom of Heaven. It is true also, that the furnishing of our rooms and cultivation of our garden is largely left to our personal industry and good taste. Still, in a general way, we must fall in with the city's plan; and consider, when we hang some new and startling curtains, how they will look from the street. However intense the personal life of each soul may be, that personal life has got out of proportion, if it makes us forget our municipal obligations and advantages; for our true significance is more than personal, it is bound up with the fact of our status as members of a super-natural society. So into all the affairs of the little house there should enter a certain sense of the city, and beyond this of the infinite world in which the city stands: some awe-struck memory of our double situation, at once so homely and so mysterious. We must each maintain unimpaired our unique relation with God; yet without forgetting our intimate contact with the rest of the city, or the mesh of invisible life which binds all the inhabitants in one.

For it is on the unchanging Life of God, as on a rock, that the whole city is founded. That august and cherishing Spirit is the atmosphere which bathes it, and fills each room of every little house—quickening, feeding and sustaining. He is the one Reality which makes us real; and, equally, the other houses too. 'If I am not in Thee,' said St. Augustine, 'then I am not at all.' We are often urged to think of the spiritual life as a personal adventure, a ceaseless hustle forward; with all its meaning condensed in the 'perfection' of the last stage. But though progress, or rather growth, is truly in it, such growth in so far as it is real can only arise from, and be conditioned by, a far more fundamental relation—the growing soul's abidingness in God.

Next, what type of house does the soul live in? It is a two-story house. The psychologist too often assumes that it is a one-roomed cottage with a mud floor; and never even attempts to go upstairs. The extreme transcendentalist sometimes talks as though it were perched in the air, like the lake dwellings of our primitive ancestors, and had no ground floor at all. A more humble attention to facts suggests that neither of these simplifications is true. We know that we have a ground floor, a natural life biologically conditioned, with animal instincts and affinities; and that this life is very important, for it is the product of the divine creativity—its builder and maker is God. But we know too that we have an upper floor, a supernatural life, with supernatural possibilities, a capacity for God; and that this, man's peculiar prerogative, is more important still. If we try to live on one floor alone we destroy the mysterious beauty of our human vocation; so utterly a part of the fugitive and creaturely life of this planet and yet so deeply coloured by Eternity; so entirely one with the world of nature, and yet, 'in the Spirit', a habitation of God. 'Thou madest him lower than the angels, to crown him with glory and worship.' We are created both in Time and in Eternity, not truly one but truly two; and every thought, word and act must be subdued to the dignity of that double situation in which Almighty God has placed and companions the childish spirit of man.

Therefore a full and wholesome spiritual life can never consist in living upstairs, and forgetting to consider the ground floor and its homely uses and needs; thus ignoring the humbling fact that those upper rooms are entirely supported by it. Nor does it consist in the constant, exasperated investigation of the shortcomings of the basement. When St. Teresa said that her prayer had become 'solid like a house', she meant that its foundations now went down into the lowly but firm ground of human nature, the concrete actualities of the natural life: and on those solid foundations, its walls rose up towards heaven. The strength of the house consisted in that intimate welding together of the divine and the human, which she found in its perfection in the humanity of Christ. There, in the common stuff of human life which He blessed by His presence, the saints have ever seen the homely foundations of holiness. Since we are two-story creatures, called to a natural and a supernatural status, both sense and spirit must be rightly maintained, kept in order, consecrated to the purposes of the city, if our full obligations are to be fulfilled. The house is built for God; to reflect, on each level, something of His unlimited Perfection. Downstairs that general rightness of adjustment to all this-world obligations, which the ancients called the quality of Justice; and the homely virtues of Prudence, Temperance and Fortitude reminding us of our creatureliness, our limitations, and so humbling and disciplining us. Upstairs, the heavenly powers of Faith, Hope and Charity; tending towards the Eternal, nourishing our life towards God, and having no meaning apart from God.

But the soul's house will never be a real home, unless the ground floor is as cared for and as habitable as the beautiful rooms upstairs. We are required to live in the whole of our premises, and are responsible for the condition of the whole of our premises. It is useless to re-paper the drawing-room, if what we really need is a new sink. In that secret Divine purpose which is drawing all life towards perfection, the whole house is meant to be beautiful and ought to be beautiful; for it comes from God, and was made to His design. Christ's soul when on earth lived in one of these houses; had to use the same fitments, make the same arrangements do. We cannot excuse our own failures by attributing them to the inconvenience of the premises, and the fact that some very old-fashioned bits of apparatus survive. Most of us have inherited some ugly bits of furniture, or unfortunate family portraits which we can't get rid of, and which prevent our rooms being quite a success. Nevertheless the soul does not grow strong merely by enjoying its upstairs privileges, and ignoring downstairs disadvantages, problems and responsibilities; but only by tackling its real task of total transformation. It is called to maintain a house which shall be in its complete-ness 'a habitation of God in the Spirit'; subdued to His purposes on all levels, manifesting His glory in what we call natural life, as well as in what we call spiritual life. For man is the link between these two orders; truly created a little lower than the angels, yet truly crowned with glory and worship, because in this unperfected human nature the Absolute Life itself has deigned to dwell.

That means, reduced to practice, that the whole house with its manifold and graded activities must be a house of prayer. It does not mean keeping a Quiet Room to which we can retreat, with mystical pictures on the walls, and curtains over the windows to temper the disconcerting intensity of the light; a room where we can forget the fact that there are black beetles in the kitchen, and that the range is not working very well. Once we admit any violent contrast between the upper and lower floor, the 'instinctive' and 'spiritual' life, or feel a reluctance to investigate the humbling realities of the basement, our life becomes less, not more, than human; and our position is unsafe. Are we capable of the adventure of courage which inspires the great prayer of St. Augustine: 'The house of my soul is narrow; do Thou enter in and enlarge it! It is ruinous; do Thou repair it?' Can we risk the visitation of the mysterious Power that will go through all our untidy rooms, showing up their short-comings and their possibilities; reproving by the tranquillity of order the waste and muddle of our inner life? The mere hoarded rubbish that ought to go into the dust-bin; the things that want mending and washing; the possessions we have never taken the trouble to use? Yet this is the only condition on which man can participate in that fullness of life for which he is made.

The Lord's Prayer, in which St. Teresa said that she found the whole art of contemplation from its simple beginning to its transcendent goal, witnesses with a wonderful beauty and completeness to this two-story character of the soul's house; and yet its absolute unity. It begins at the top, in the watch tower of faith, with the sublime assertion of our supernatural status—the one relation, intimate yet inconceivable, that governs all the rest—'Our Father who art in Heaven, hallowed be *Thy* name.' Whatever the downstairs muddle and tension we have to deal with, however great the difficulty of adjusting the claims of the instincts that live in the basement and the interests that clamour at the door, all these demands, all this rich and testing experience, is enfolded and transfused by the cherishing, over-ruling life and power of God. ❦ We are lifted clear of the psychological tangle in which the life of our spirit too often seems enmeshed, into the pure, serene light of Eternity; and shown the whole various and disconcerting pageant of creation as proceeding from God, and existing only that it may glorify His name. Childlike dependence and joyful adoration are placed together as the twin characters of the soul's relation to God.

Thence, step by step, this prayer brings us downstairs, goes with us through the whole house; bringing the supernatural into the natural, blessing and sanctifying, cleansing and rectifying every aspect of the home. '*Thy Kingdom* come!' Hope—trustful expectation. '*Thy will* be done!' Charity—the loving union of our wills with the Infinite Will. Then the ground floor. 'Give us this day'—that food from beyond ourselves which nourishes and sustains our life. Forgive all our little failures and excesses, neutralize the corroding power of our conflicts, disharmonies, rebellions, sins. We can't deal with them alone. Teach us, as towards our fellow citizens, to share that generous tolerance of God. Lead us not into situations where we are tried beyond our strength; but meet us on the battlefield of personality, and protect the weakness of the adolescent spirit against the downward pull of the inhabitants of the lower floor.

And then, the reason of all this; bringing together, in one supreme declaration of joy and confidence, the soul's sense of that supporting, holy, and eternal Reality who is the Ruler and the Light of the city, and of every room in every little house. *Thine* is the Kingdom, the Power

71

and the Glory. If our interior life be subdued to the spirit of this prayer, with its rich sense of our mighty heritage and child-like status, our total dependence on the Reality of God, then the soul's house is truly running well. Its action is transfused by contemplation. The door is open between the upper and the lower floor; the life of spirit and life of sense.

'Two cities,' said St. Augustine, 'have been created by two loves: the earthly city by love of self even to contempt of God, the heavenly city by love of God even to contempt of self. The one city glories in itself; the other city glories in the Lord. The one city glories in its own strength; the other city says to its God, '"I will love Thee, O Lord my strength."' Perhaps there has never been a time in Christian history when that contrast has been more sharply felt than it is now—the contrast between that view of man's situation and meaning, in which the emphasis falls on humanity, its vast desires and wonderful achievements, even to contempt of God; and the view in which the emphasis falls on God's transcendent action and over-ruling will, even to contempt of self. St. Augustine saw, and still would see, mankind ever at work building those two cities; and every human soul as a potential citizen of one or the other. And from this point of view, that which we call the 'interior life' is just the home life of those who inhabit the invisible City of God: realistically taking up their municipal privileges and duties, and pursuing them 'even to contempt of self'. It is the obligation and the art of keeping the premises entrusted to us in good order; having ever in view the welfare of the city as a whole.

Some souls, like some people, can be slummy anywhere. There is always a raucous and uncontrolled voice ascending from the basement, and a pail of dirty water at the foot of the stairs. Others can achieve in the most impossible situation a simple and beautiful life. The good citizen must be able without reluctance to open the door at all times, not only at the week-end; must keep the windows clean and taps running properly, that the light and living water may come in. These free gifts of the supernatural are offered to each house; and only as free gifts can they be had. Our noisy little engine will not produce the true light; nor our most desperate digging a proper water supply. Recognition of this fact, this entire dependence of the creature, is essential if the full benefits of our mysterious citizenship are ever to be enjoyed by us. 'I saw,' said the poet of the Apocalypse, 'the holy city coming *down* from God out of heaven . . . the glory of God lit it . . . the water of life proceeded out of the throne of God.' All is the free gift of the supernatural; not the result of human growth and effort. God's generous and life-giving work in the world of souls ever goes before man's work in God. So the main thing about the Invisible City is not the industry and good character of the inhabitants: they do not make it shine. It is the tranquil operation of that perpetual providence, which incites and supports their small activities; the direct and child-like relation in which they stand to the city's Ruler; the generous light and air that bathe the little houses; the unchanging rock of Eternity on which their foundations stand.

II

WE come back to examine more closely our domestic
responsibilities: the two floors of the soul's house. We
begin on the ground floor; for until that is in decent
order, it is useless to go upstairs. A well-ordered natural
life is the only safe basis of our supernatural life: Christianity, which brought the ground floor, with its powerful
but unruly impulses, within the area of God's grace,
demands its sublimation and dedication to His purposes.
We are required to live in the whole of our house, learning to go freely and constantly up and down stairs
backwards and forwards, easily and willingly, from one
kind of life to the other; weaving together the higher
and lower powers of the soul, and using both for the
glory of God. No exclusive spirituality will serve the
purposes of man, called to be a link between two worlds.

There are days, months—for some there will be years—
when we look out of the window of faith, and find that
the view is hidden in a mantle of fog: when we turn to
the workshop of hope, and find the fog has made that
chill and gloomy too: when we resort to the central
heating, and find that is not working very well. Then
when Faith, Hope and Charity all seem to fail us—is the
time to remember the excellent advice which Mrs. Berry
gave to Richard Feverel's bride: 'When the parlour fire
burns low, put on coals in the kitchen.' Accept your
limitations, go downstairs, and attend to the life of the
lower floor. Our vocation requires of us an equal

alertness with the censer and the scrubbing brush. When the door between the two storys is open, a flood of disconcerting light is shed upon that lower floor and its condition; and our feeble excuses for its muddled state fade into silence. But if we face the facts in the right spirit we shall find, like St. Teresa, the Presence we lost upstairs walking among the pots and pans.

The disciplined use of the lower floor and all the rich material it offers is therefore essential to the peace and prosperity of the upper floor; we cannot merely shut the door at the top of the basement stairs and hope for the best. The loud voices of unmortified nature, saying 'I want! I will! I won't!' rising up from the kitchen premises, will ruin the delicate music of the upstairs wireless. Here is the source of all the worst distractions in prayer, and the lair of all the devils that tempt us most: our inclinations to selfish choices, inordinate enjoyments, claimful affection, self-centred worry, instinctive avoidance of sacrifice and pain—all the downward drag of animal life. Here, as St. Teresa says in *The Interior Castle*, we are likely to find damp unpleasant corners; and reptiles and other horrors lurking in them. If the house is to be well run, we must begin by cleaning the kitchen and the scullery; and giving their energetic but unruly inhabitants their jobs. The human power of choice must be submitted to the rule of Prudence; human impulse and desire to the rule of Temperance; our self-protecting mechanisms, sloth, softness, nervous fears, to the bracing touch of Fortitude. That threefold reordering and sublimation of the ground floor—drastic but unsensational—will test and purify the soul's realism, humility and love, far more fully, will subdue it to the mysterious Divine action far more completely, than any hasty retreat upstairs can do. 'Not only a good way, but the best of ways,' says St. Teresa, 'is to strive to enter

75

first by the room where humility is practised, which is far better than at once rushing on to the others.'

It was no mere upstairs mystic, exclusively absorbed in spiritual things, who uttered the mysterious and haunting words 'To me, to live is Christ'. It was St. Paul, wrestling with his own difficult nature, and perpetually conscious of the conflict between sense and spirit as he lived towards God. Here and now, on the ground floor, to live with Prudence, Temperance and Fortitude in the circumstances given me, and with the temperament and furniture given me—because that ground floor is crowned and blessed by the life of Faith, Hope and Charity tending towards God—*this* 'is Christ'. There is not one landlord for the lower floor, and another for the upstairs flat.

Every soul, says that true psychologist Augustine Baker, has two internal lights or guides, the spirit of Nature and the Spirit of God: and besides these 'we neither have nor can have, any other within us'. We are reminded of that familiar picture of the old-fashioned nursery—the child with a good angel at the right hand and a bad angel at the left. Like many other bits of childish mythology, that picture points beyond itself to a deep truth. The good angel is really there: *Anima*, the soul's being when it ascends to its apex, as the mystics say, stands in the watch tower of faith, opens the window towards Eternity, beholds the Light that is God. 'The Supream part of the Soul,' says Peter Sterry, 'which is above Sensible Things, ever living in the midst of Invisible Things—this is each Man's Angel.' And the bad angel is really there too—this same complex and variable soul, when it capitulates to the unfortunate influences of the scullery. We know too well that, like the dog who has been trained to the drawing-room, there still remains something in us which takes a sneaking interest in the dustbin and will drift off in that direction if given a chance. The first thing we realize when we achieve any genuine self-knowledge, is the existence of those two levels or aspects of the soul's life: the natural self subject to mutability, the secret and essential self capable of reality, tending to God. They often seem to pull different ways; the unstable will can hardly keep its feet between them. If we consider in this light the last unfortunate episode which showed us up to ourselves; when we made the second-best choice, when a sudden tug at our elbow assured us that this particular bit of magnanimity, that renunciation, was really too much to expect—even though it shone with an unearthly radiance, though *Anima* said 'Follow me!'—then the force of the ancient Advent prayer comes home to us. 'O Wisdom proceeding out of the mouth of the Most High, come and teach me the way of Prudence' between the two conflicting aspects of my double life.

Prudence, on the natural level so suggestive of a self-centred carefulness, the miserable policy of 'safety first', only achieves dignity and beauty when thus raised to the spiritual status, and related to our life in God. Then it is revealed as the virtue which governs and sublimates all behaviour; as Temperance is the virtue which governs and sublimates desire. We owe to St. Thomas the noblest and deepest of all definitions of Prudence. For him, all virtues, all the soul's sources of energy, are forms and expressions of one thing—Love, the self's will and desire, in the ascending degrees of preference, interest, longing and devotedness, set towards God and the will of God. And conversely, all sin is due to something gone wrong with that same sacred power of energetic love; its direction to wrong objectives. Sin is 'a withdrawal from the art of Divine Wisdom and the order of Divine Love': a wilful setting of our own small lives, hopes and loves out of line with the vast purposes of God. The right ordering of its innate powers of love and will is therefore all the soul has to do to actualize its inheritance, make it fit for God. *Ordina quest' amore, o tu che m'ami.* Then, the soul's house is ready for its guest. And Prudence, says St. Thomas again, is this Love 'choosing between what helps and what hinders'—choosing what helps the fulfilment of God's will, and leaving what hinders the fulfilment of that will; because He is the soul's love. It is the dedicated use of the great human power of choice, its subjection to the rule of charity: the right ordering of the natural life in the interests, not of one's own preference or advancement, but of the city and the city's King.

Thus Prudence is like a good housekeeper; not very attractive at first sight, but a valuable sort of woman to put in charge if you want your soul's house to be well run. With her eye on efficiency, but always for love's sake, she will use her resources in the best way, keep up the premises, provide regular and suitable meals. She will not serve devotional meringues for breakfast, or try to make beautiful fluffy omelettes full of fervour just when eggs are scarce. Dealing with her situation as it really is, and not proceeding on the assumption that it really ought to be something else, more interesting, exalted and flattering to self-love, she will be provident: not using up all her resources at the beginning of the week, or making plans she cannot carry out. She will refuse to translate the words 'called to be saints' into 'called to behave as if we were already saints'. She will balance prayer and action, never giving out beyond her power, or forgetting to get in fresh supplies: so that her spiritual store cupboard is never bare. How mortified, free from all spiritual fancifulness and extravagance, is a life over which Prudence presides; love of God, even to contempt of self, determining all choices, purifying all motives, and maintaining an orderly, disciplined life in the soul.

We find this science of behaviour operative in both the great aspects of our human experience, the outward and the inward: our behaviour towards other souls, our behaviour to ourselves. As regards others, it will mean the loving and careful choice of all that helps and does not hinder *them*. In the life of action, the mortified use of our rightful initiative. In the life of feeling, the custody of the heart, in the interests of our neighbour's peace as well as our own. In the life of thought, a humble avoidance of comments on the crude and childish nature of the symbols through which other souls reach out to God; a discreet suppression of that clever and interesting bit of up-to-date theology, those startling ethical ideas, which flatter our intelligence but may disturb more tender-minded souls. Nothing is more marked in the Gospels than the prudence with which Christ gave spiritual truths from His infinite store: always enlightening, but never overwhelming the homely, sense-conditioned human creatures to whom He was sent. The Mind which saw God, and all things displayed in the light of the Divine Wisdom, and which longed to give all men that great vision which is beatitude, came down from nights of communion with that Reality upon the mountain, to teach with Prudence. 'Without a parable spake He not'—and those parables were made of the homeliest materials, with little to attract a fastidious spirituality. Yet in them the secret of the Kingdom was hid, so that only those who were ready for the teaching received it. Perfect Wisdom came with kindergarten methods to men's kindergarten souls.

The mind awakened to spiritual reality often needs much self-control, much prudence, if it is to put the truth it has acquired—usually very little—so generally and so genially that there is no risk of giving anyone a spiritual shock, or the chance of spiritual gastritis. All teachers have to learn with St. Paul to subordinate their own vision to their pupils' needs; feeding babies with milk because they need milk, whilst suppressing the disheartening information that there is a more complete diet in the cupboard. Prudence proves her love as much by what she withholds as by what she gives: humbly and patiently adapting her method to the capacity of each. She never bewilders, dazzles, little growing souls; never over-feeds or drags them out of their depth. The cakes upon her tea-table are suited to the digestion of the guests.

Prudence further requires the careful handling of our own lives and capacities; instruments given us by God, and destined to be mirrors of His skill. It means choosing what helps, and rejecting what hinders, the fulfilment of that design, that vocation, which is already present in embryo in our souls. This subjection of behaviour to the ultimate purpose of God may mean on one hand conduct which seems absurdly over-careful; or on the other, conduct which seems imprudent to the last degree. The truly prudent, love-impelled choices of the saints, are often in the eyes of the world the extreme of foolishness. St. Simon Stylites, making his pillar higher and higher in his quest of that solitude to which he knew that he was called; St. Francis stripping off all that impeded his love, even to his very clothes, and going out to destitution; St. Catherine of Genoa, forcing herself to repulsive duties because they helped to kill fastidiousness, and make her self-oblivious love more complete; Father Damien, choosing the certitude of a leper's death; Father Wainwright, deliberately going without a midday meal for years, because love made him want to share the privations of those he served—all these are the actions of celestial prudence. Prudence, not preference, took St. Teresa to the convent. She did not like the cloister, but she knew herself called by God; and chose that which helped to fulfil His will for her soul. Prudence locked the door of Lady Julian's cell, but sent Mary Slessor from the Scottish mill to the African jungle; took Foucauld to the solitude of the Sahara, Livingstone to Africa, Grenfell to Labrador.

Love chooses the work it can do, not the work that it likes. Prudent love took St. Thomas from contemplation, and made him the teacher of the schools. Prudent love does not insist on being a philanthropist when it lacks the warm outgoing temperament that is needed, and is decisively called to the more lonely but not less essential vocation of studying the deep things of God. It uses the material given it in the best possible way; and thus doing, makes its appointed contribution to that eternal plan which requires the perfect active surrender of the willing creature, the making of all choices and performance of all tasks in subservience to that God Who is Pure Act— the total consecration of natural life. 'We are always,' says De Caussade, 'running after some chimerical perfection, and losing sight of the only rule of real perfection, which is the will of God—that infinitely wise and infinitely gentle will, which if we make it our guide, will show us near at hand at any moment, that which we vainly and laboriously seek elsewhere.'

In the *Paradiso* Dante, with his usual acuteness, makes Prudence—love choosing rightly—the boundary between perfect and imperfect beatitude. The Heaven of those active saints through whom the Divine Wisdom is imparted to men, is the Heaven of Prudence. Minds widely separated in temper and outlook, but united by their loving choice of God—Anselm and Chrysostom, Francis and Dominic, Hugh of St. Victor and Thomas Aquinas—there dwell together. It is there that the music of eternity first becomes audible by human ears.

And this is surely right; for it is only by means of those costly, love-impelled choices which are the essence of heavenly Prudence, that the natural creature can enter more and more fully into the rhythm of the supernatural life.

For in the governance of our natural lives, a genuine choice is left to us. We are neither dummies, nor the slaves of circumstance. We are living creatures possessed of a limited freedom, a power of initiative, which increases every time we use it the right way; we are trained and developed by being confronted with alternatives, on which tremendous issues hang. It is typical of the completeness with which each essential factor of our human experience finds its rule and pattern in the Gospels, that this free choice between possible courses should form our Lord's actual preparation for His public ministry. Enlightened at baptism as to His divine Sonship, His unique commission, He did not at once rush off 'in the power of the Spirit' to preach the good news. 'He who believeth shall not make haste.' Real power is the result of inner harmony, and requires perfect accord between the upper and the lower floors; impulse harnessed to obedience. Therefore the Spirit of Wisdom drove Him into the wilderness, to come to terms with His own human nature. More than one path lay open before Him. He might claim the privileges of an exceptional spirit, in the midst of a world which is not exceptional at all: turn the material world to His own purpose, transcend the common laws of nature, assume the position of the Father's pet child. He might follow the path disclosed by spiritual ambition, leading to obvious power and success: the most insidious of the three temptations, because it suggested that His mission of redemption and enlightenment could be fulfilled on a great scale, by entering into alliance with the spirit and methods of the world. People who think

in numbers always mistake this for a call from God.
Love, choosing what helped, rejected all these opportunities, and elected the humble career of a local prophet
and evangelist: a limited scope, unrewarded service, an
unappreciative public, a narrow path leading to the
Cross.

The spiritual life constantly offers its neophytes the
equivalent of all these temptations. There are those
who think first of their own spiritual hunger, and the
imperative duty of feeding their own souls: those for
whom the spiritual life means spiritual privilege—who
defy common sense, take foolish risks, and call the
proceeding trust in God: those who accept methods of
recommending religion which are something less than
spiritual, and call this 'dealing with the conditions of
modern life'. All these courses in their different ways
may seem prudent; and all wilt away before the selfless
prudence of Christ. That picture, in its austere majesty
and loneliness, forces the soul to consider how much
disguised self-interest, how much irresponsibility, how
much inclination to compromise, hang about its ground
floor and impede the purity of its choice for God. For
the inner spring which governs all truly prudent choice
is such a generous, general and self-oblivious surrender
as over-rules mere personal preference, can envisage with
equal calmness apparent failure and apparent success,
and ignores even its own spiritual advantage. The New
Testament contains no single instance in which our
Lord sought or obtained a private spiritual advantage:
and the devout persons who do so are at best only vege-
table-fibre saints. Like artificial silk, they look very
glossy, but do not stand much wear and tear.

Now Prudence is a positive, not a negative, principle
of action. It requires behaviour, not abstention from
behaviour. It rejects the lower, in order that it may be

83

free to accept the higher choice. Thus our dominant attraction is in the eyes of Prudence as important as our dominant temptation: it may be the magnet by which we are being drawn to the place we have to fill. The creative method completes detachment by attachment: 'Leave all' requires as its corollary 'Follow me'. It may therefore be a work of Prudence to make tentative advances along a path which attracts us; whether of prayer, study, active work, human love or renunciation. But when God, speaking through circumstances, says 'That way is not open'; then it is for us humbly to acquiesce, whatever the cost. Love must learn by experience to recognize when the secret inward pressure comes from God, and when it really comes from self-will, and we persuade ourselves that it is the push of God. Nothing is more important than that we should faithfully follow our own true spiritual attraction; develop and use the talent given into our care. But it needs a humble and a prudent spirit to discover what that is, and distinguish it from the other more exciting kind of attraction which is really rooted in self-love.

To do this is the work of Discretion, the handmaid of Prudence: and the test that she proposes is simple enough. 'If God be thy love and thy meaning, the choice and point of thy heart,' says the author of *The Cloud of Unknowing*, 'it sufficeth to thee in this life.' There, in a phrase, is the heart of Heavenly Prudence. It requires a total transformation of our attitude towards existence; because the choice and point of our heart is set towards the Eternal, our love and our meaning is God, and we are running our house for Him. If we test by this standard the dubious choices we have made, the chances we have missed, the responsibilities we have dodged, we shall perceive in each of them a virtual confession that the

84

Living Perfect and its interests were not really the choice and point of our heart. Easy paths taken, awkward paths left; a cowardly inclination to take shelter behind circumstances. In personal relationships, a quiet avoidance of the uncongenial, a certain blindness to opportunities for exercising generous love. In religion, perverse insistence on particular notions and practices; self-chosen adventures in devotional regions to which we were not decisively called. Prudence, remembering the modest size of her own premises and the sublimity of those experiences of God which the mystics try with stammering tongues to suggest, will always choose a simple type of prayer suited to her capacity, and never attempt that which is beyond her powers; for she has no spiritual ambition, beyond faithful correspondence with God. How sober, mortified, truly discreet is the prayer of the saints; faithful, loyal, free from self-chosen peculiarities, keeping steadily on through darkness and through light.

So too the detachment to which Prudence will urge us, will not merely consist in cutting out those things and persons which attract us, and are occasions of temptation and unrest: thus eliminating the very material of self-discipline from life. It will rather require the practice of detachment in attachment; using with love the educational toys in our cupboard, but refusing to make them into idols or break into angry howls when they are taken away. Prudence requires love without claimfulness, and service without self-will; cherishing and studying the people placed within our radius, but even here, never seeking our own along the subtle paths of spiritual friendship. She demands a life that is both world-embracing and world-renouncing in its amplitude of surrendered love. This means a constant and difficult tension; many falls, perhaps continuous suffering, perpetual slaps

85

to affection and pride. Again and again the unruly lower nature seems to be conquered; again and again it catches us out. It is one thing to make Love's choice, and quite another to stick to it. Nevertheless this is the right way to handle the ground floor life; not eliminating its frictions, but using its capacities, and gradually purifying the use of them from self-love. We can afford to have a warm and well-furnished kitchen, and even to take pride in it, so long as we remember that it *is* a kitchen; and that all its activities must be subservient to the interests of the whole house, and its observance of the city's law.

III

IF it is the special work of Prudence to manage our basement premises, so run the domestic life of the soul that all its willed choices, the trend of its behaviour, subserve the purposes of God; it is the special work of Temperance to harness and control the natural instincts, and subdue them to the same end. Temperance, says St. Thomas, is the Virtue of the Beautiful, the virtue which tempers and orders our vehement desires, and subjects even our apparently spiritual cravings to the mortifying action of love: for moderation, proportion, reverence for conditions, is the very secret of a lasting beauty. To worship the Lord in the beauty of holiness does not mean the unbridled enthusiasm of the dervish, but the quiet and steadfast loyalty of the saint.

Temperance, then, must preside over the furnishing of the soul's house, if it is to be the setting of a useful, ordered, peaceful interior life. Much discipline, moderation, actual self-denial are involved in wise furnishing. No hurried purchase of the cheap or attractive, without considering the size and shape of our rooms; no copying of our neighbour's interesting new curtains, oblivious of the fact that they will never live with our dear old rugs; no frenzied efforts to get a grand piano into a two-roomed flat. If the house is to be a success, what we leave out will be quite as important as what we put in. *Abstine et sustine.* At every turn we are required to reconsider our first notions, accept our limitations, mortify our

87

desires. It is useless to begin in a style that we cannot keep up; or, when we see what it involves, will want to keep up. We all know rooms full of little vases, faded photographs, plush elephants, and shabby books of verse; relics of the owners' transient and uncontrolled impulses. Those rooms lack all sense of space, tranquillity and dignity; because Temperance, the strong virtue of the Beautiful, has not been called in. So too the furnishing of the soul's house depends for its success on a wise austerity. It requires a spirit of renunciation; checking that love of what is new, odd or startling, which so easily kills the taste for quiet colour and simple things, that tendency to accumulate odds and ends which swamps our few real treasures in a dusty crowd of devotional nick-nacks. The inner life does not consist in the abundance and peculiarity of our spiritual possessions. There is nothing so foolish, snobbish, and in the end so disastrous as trying to furnish beyond our means; forgetting our creaturely status, and the very moderate position which our small house occupies in the City of God.

Again, Temperance will lay a restraining hand on the speculative instinct, when it is tempted to rush off to the horizons of thought or make fatuous efforts to achieve a 'concept of God'; forgetting, in its immoderate craving for sharper outlines or more light, the awful disparity between the infinite mystery and the useful but limited human mind, and the fact that it is under human conditions, in a human world, that God desires to maintain and transfigure the soul. 'The angels feed on Thee fully,' says the ancient prayer of the priest before Mass: 'Let pilgrim man feed on Thee according to his measure.'

Christianity insists that all we need and can assimilate will be given to us at home; the Light of the human world coming to us here and now, as the Bread of Life. But it takes a temperate soul to savour all that lies hidden

88

in this saying—its moderation, homeliness, perfect adaptation to our creaturely needs. True, the heavens declare the glory of the Lord; but we, whirling along on our tiny bit of heaven, are more overwhelmed than illuminated by that majestic revelation. We remain merely dazzled and bewildered till we consent to come off our high horse, get our feet firmly on the earth, and look here and now for the life-giving Reality mediated through earthly things. 'I am the Son of man, that two-storied, half-made creature. I do not despise the ground floor and its needs. I am the Bread of his little life, the Light of his little world: yet I and my Father are one.'

Thus the characteristic mode of God's self-giving to the human soul is declared to be something which we can best compare to our ordinary necessary daily food; given to us right down in the common life, and satisfying a fundamental need which is independent of feeling and taste. Man lives on God, is 'renewed day by day by the Spirit'; by regular plain meals, offered and deliberately taken here and now, not by occasional moments of ecstatic communion. By solid food, not spiritual sweets. 'He gave them *bread* from Heaven to eat.' Only a soul disciplined to temperance can relish all that there is to be found in bread. Its excursions and aspirations, its delighted ascents to God, if legitimate and wholesome, must always bring it back to discover more savour and meaning in this plain, homely Bread of Life.

'You seek,' says De Caussade, 'the secret of union with God. There is no other secret but to make use of the material God gives us.' That material is mixed, like the environment in which we find ourselves. Temperance will teach us to accept it as it comes to us—not arrogantly ignoring the visible in our search for the invisible, but remembering that the life of the city enfolds and penetrates both. Here the greatest mystics have been

G

89

the most temperate, and so most closely in touch with the spirit of the New Testament. St. Francis finds in the difficulties and humiliations of normal existence the essence of perfect joy. St. Térèsa 'desires no other prayer than that which makes her a better woman'. The latest in time of her daughters, St. Therese of Lisieux, esteems 'one sacrifice better than any ecstasy'. Brother Lawrence is content to do his cooking in the Presence of God. St. François de Sales, when St. Chantal tries to turn the conversation to spiritual channels, directs her attention to the little tune the footman is singing outside the door. For all of these the landlord of the upper floor is the landlord of the ground floor too.

Temperance, then, is the teacher of that genial humility which is an essential of spiritual health. It makes us realize that the normal and moderate course is the only one we can handle successfully in our own power: that extraordinary practices, penances, spiritual efforts, with their corresponding graces, must never be deliberately sought. Some people appear to think that the 'spiritual life' is a peculiar condition mainly supported by cream ices and corrected by powders. But the solid norm of the spiritual life should be like that of the natural life: a matter of porridge, bread and butter, and a cut off the joint. The extremes of joy, discipline, vision, are not in our hands, but in the Hand of God. We can maintain the soul's house in order without any of these. It is not the best housekeeper who has the most ferocious spring-clean, or gets in things from the confectioner when she is expecting guests. 'If any man open the door, I will come in to him'; share his ordinary meal, and irradiate his ordinary life. The demand for temperance of soul, for an acknowledgement of the sacred character of the normal, is based on that fact—the central Christian fact—of the humble entrance of God into our common human life. The supernatural can and does seek and find us, in and through our daily normal experience: the invisible in the visible. There is no need to be peculiar in order to find God. The Magi were taught by the heavens to follow a star; and it brought them, not to a paralysing disclosure of the Transcendent, but to a little Boy on His mother's knee.

So too we observe how moderate, humble, attuned to the scale of our daily life are all the crucial events of the New Testament. Seen from the outside, none could have guessed their shattering and transfiguring power. The apocalyptists looked for a superhuman being 'coming in the clouds'—they could not escape from the idea of the abnormal—but the real events which transformed the spiritual history of man were startling only in their simplicity. The quiet routine of a childhood and working life in Nazareth; the wandering ministry of teaching and compassion, with the least possible stress laid on super-natural powers; the homely little triumph of Palm Sunday; the pitiful sufferings of an arrest and execution too commonplace to disturb the city's life. Christ never based His claim on strangeness: it is by what He is, rather than by what He does, that He awes, attracts, amazes.

In spite of its contrasts between the stern and tender, how steadily temperate and central in its emphasis is all His teaching: full of the colour and quality of real life free from the merely startling, ever keeping close to our normal experience. Sowing, reaping, bread-making, keeping sheep; in these the secrets of the Kingdom are hid. He does not ask His disciples to speculate on the Divine Nature, but to consider the lilies; it comes to the same thing and is more suited to our powers. He looks at and studies these simple and natural things with the eyes of sympathetic love; because for Him the super-natural indwells and supports all natural things, not

91

merely abnormal or 'religious' things. Therefore each and all of these natural things, made by God and kept by God, can become supernatural revelations of His Spirit. We feel our Lord's complete understanding of the thing-world in all its richness, beauty and pathos, His careful, reverent, tender observation of animals, birds and plants: yet, His entire aloofness from its clutch, the deep harmony of His Spirit with the very Spirit of Creative Love. No cleavage here between the two levels of man's life: the spirit of the upper floor penetrates to every corner, and transfuses alike the most sacred and homely activities.

The discourse in the 12th chapter of St. Luke is full of this temperate genial attitude to the natural, in its contrast with that intemperance of soul which alternates between an absolute and inhuman detachment and using the world of things in a childish grasping way. It is a long varied lesson in the true realism. Consider that wonderful world of life in which you are placed, and observe that its great rhythms of birth, growth and death —all the things that really matter—are not in your control. That unhurried process will go forward in its stately beauty, little affected by your anxious fuss. Find out, then, where your treasure really is. Discern substance from accident. Don't confuse your meals with your life, and your clothes with your body. Don't lose your head over what perishes. Nearly everything does perish: so face the facts, don't rush after the transient and unreal. Maintain your soul in tranquil dependence on God; don't worry; don't mistake what you possess for what you are. Accumulating things is useless. Both mental and material avarice are merely silly in view of the dread facts of life and death. The White Knight would have done better had he left his luggage at home. The simpler your house, the easier it will be to run. The fewer the things and the people you 'simply must have', the nearer you will be to the ideal of happiness—'as having nothing, to possess all'. We observe how exquisitely the whole doctrine is kept within the boundaries of our natural experience: how it tends to deepen this given experience rather than escape from it. Man is being taught how to run that ground-floor life which he cannot get rid of and must not ignore; yet taught by one in whom the other life shines with unmatched perfection, whose whole personality radiates God.

If now we consider how we ourselves stand in respect of this virtue of Temperance, we discover that it must bring its sobering realism into our social, personal, and spiritual life. Its peaceful acceptance of facts must colour all our relations with others, all our dealings with ourselves, all our responses to God.

First, in relation to others Temperance requires a quiet refusal to capitulate to feverish and distracting emotions; intense attractions and intense hostilities. It means a tempering of ground-floor passions to the needs of the upstairs life; that check upon vehement impulse, that ordering of love, which involves its absolute dissociation from claimfulness, clutch and excess. The love which the Saints pour out is a gentle and genial sunshine; never fierce, concentrated, intemperate. Those who come to the soul's house should find it nicely warmed all over; its inner chamber must not be like one of those rooms which have a fierce little gas stove in one corner, and a deadly chill everywhere else. *Custodia cordis*, the secret of an ordered life, involves the maintenance of an even temperature; and a refusal to rush out upon a flood of inordinate feeling towards certain persons, deeds and things, instead of taking what comes to us tranquilly, with a light hand.

Again, theological views, and political loyalties, must

all be subject to the rule of temperance; killing presumption, intolerance and the spirit of controversy, acknowledging at each point the fragmentary and relative character of all human knowledge and therefore the peril and absurdity of absolute judgements and scornful criticisms of the opinions of other men. So too the restless, energetic desire to get things done, the impetuous determination to remodel the world nearer to our own hearts' desire, the exaggerated importance we attribute to our own action, the emphasis placed on doing, to the detriment of being—all this must be mortified if calm and order are to rule the lower floor. We shall never create a home-like atmosphere unless we consent to spend some time in our own home; and, were a better balance struck between our inward life and our outward activities, the result would at once be seen in the improved quality of that outward work. Like Peter's wife's mother, while the fever is on us we cannot really serve our fellow men.

I often think that when St. Paul wrote his classic list of the fruits of the Spirit, he gave us unconsciously a wonderful account of his own growth in this spiritual realism. We should hardly think of the virtue of Temperance as specially characteristic of St. Paul, and even to the end of his days he probably found it difficult; yet in this he discovers the final proof of the working of Creative Spirit in his soul. He begins upon a note of convinced fervour. 'The fruit—the harvest—of the Spirit is Love, Joy, Peace.' No three words could better express that rich beatitude which, in his holiest moments, has flooded his soul. Then he pauses. We seem to see him thinking, 'After all, I don't always feel like that. Things are often very trying. I don't seem able to love; peace and joy are unobtainable; I feel another law in my members warring against the law of my mind. Yet the indwelling Spirit is still there: to live *is* Christ. How does that

94

Spirit act on my troubled spirit in those less expansive moments? Surely in the long-suffering, gentleness and kindness which I know must control all my reactions to the world of men.' They were not the reactions which St. Paul found specially easy. We see the yoke being laid on his stormy instinctive nature: the love that is easy on the upper floor being brought downstairs, to prove itself in the common life.

At last, at the very end, we reach those unexpected characters which are the earnest of his total transformation in the Spirit. Fidelity, Meekness, Moderation: an unsensational but unbroken loyalty to the infinite life and purpose which had made him its own, an acceptance of its gradual pace, a refusal to hurry, a restraining of the impetuous desire to get everything possible out of those new converts who were only babies still, and tell the candid truth to those who had let him down—these are the real fruits of his subjection to God. Paul, whose first idea had been to breathe fire and slaughter upon the Christians, and whose second idea had been to be 'all out' for Christ—who was quite as obsessed as we are by the vision of all that there was to do, and the sense that he was called upon to do it—learns that the final gift of the Spirit is not intensity of life, but Temperance. 'The servant of the Lord must not strive.' Hurry, bustle, anxiety to get things done; an immoderate demand for perfection and consequent nervous wear and tear; the wasteful use of the premises given us by God, are all condemned.

Next, we are called to be temperate as regards the standard by which we estimate ourselves; which must neither be too degraded nor too exalted for our status. We are neither angels nor devils, but half-achieved, unstable creatures; alternately pulled towards the higher and the lower life. Temperance, therefore, will not take

95

too ferocious a view of our inevitable fluctuations. It will not judge the state of our house by its ground floor alone or its upper rooms alone; but by both. The ground floor, to the very end, will partake of the imperfection of nature. It is good and humbling that this should be so: and we should bring a certain genial patience to acceptance of the facts, bearing evenly our own uneven performances. Our part is to manage the household wisely, without overstraining its resources; if we do, it will have its revenge. So we are required to be reasonable both in what we refuse to nature and what we demand from it; temperate in renunciation as well as enjoyment, in supersensible as well as sensible activities. The spiritual life constantly draws upon the resources of the natural life; much nervous energy is used in prayer, especially absorbed or difficult prayer. Therefore we should treat our limited powers with reverence, avoiding wasteful overstrain. Further, we should arrange our housework on a reasonable plan: not letting ourselves in for a whole day's scrubbing, and then in our desperation resorting to strong soda and harsh soap. After all, the interior life needs no sensational measures. It requires only our gentle and faithful collaboration with God, in fitting the human nature He has given us for Him; gradually making the whole house ready for that Spirit which is tranquillity and peace.

Thus temperance in regard to ourselves involves temperance as towards God; an avoidance of the devotional strain and clutch we sometimes mistake for fervour; a humble recognition of our limits in respect of that communion with Him which we can enjoy. The beginning of all spiritual wisdom is a realization of the moderate character of our situation—the vast distance between even the most illuminated soul and those mysteries of the Being of God on which the seraphs did not dare to look.

Temperance suggests to us how awe-struck and humble, how full of adoration our demeanour should be, over against that unsearchable Reality; how moderate and child-like our choice of religious objectives and practices. We are not to 'ransack the Divine Majesty' as the old mystics had it, but meekly accept the revelation of Himself that He gives us; never arrogantly seeking more light than we can bear, or more food than we can digest.

'Well, Sadie,' said an American mother to her little girl, who was devouring everything within reach, 'I reckon you won't long have the use of that breakfast.' There are intemperate devotional meals to which the same risk is attached. It is left to us to feed our souls wisely and carefully—not too many spiritual sweets, not too much effervescent emotion. We are to be content with the food we find suits us—strengthens us, makes us grow—not make wild efforts to get the food we like best. Nor are we to be fastidious in our rejection of everything we do not think 'essential', until we reach what we choose to regard as a 'purely spiritual' type of prayer. Our ghostly insides are much like our natural insides; they need a certain amount of what doctors call 'roughage', and seldom thrive on too refined a diet.

The homely mixed food, the routine meals, of institutional religion, keep our digestions in good order. Particularly at times when we are drawn to fervour, or our spiritual sensibility seems to transcend the average level, we need the wholesome corrective of the common religious diet, the average practice, with its rough and ready adaptation to ordinary needs and limitations, to remind us that we are not pure spirits yet. In that excellent parable, *The History of Sir John Sparrow*, a logical insistence on the reduction of his food to its essential constituents at last left the hero face to face with a saucer of canary seed. He had proved that it contained all the human body needed; but somehow the position was not a satisfactory one. Therefore Temperance will restrain us from simplifying or etherealizing our religious diet over-much. We are mixed feeders, and must do as our fellows. Fastidious choices, special paths, look rather ridiculous in the 'perpetual bright clearness of Eternity'.

The light which bathes the paintings of the Umbrian masters, and gives them their profound tranquillity, is not a vivid illumination. It reveals no distant detail, creates no violent contrasts. Yet we feel that its gentle radiance, softening all harsh outlines, comes from beyond the world in its unearthly beauty; and quietens everything on which it falls. It stills all passion and intensity, reproves all haste: gives the calm beauty of holiness even to the anguish of the Cross. That is the light in which the soul's life, world, prayer, should be bathed: harmonizing nature and spirit in its lovely, temperate radiance. The Heaven of Temperance, says Dante, is the home of the contemplative saints. In its soil the ladder is planted on which they ascend to the Vision of God. For Temperance, stilling those excesses of desire, those self-actuated struggles, which hinder the silent working of Creative Spirit in the soul, finds its perfect work in that quietude, humility and suppleness which are the only preparation of prayer.

IV

WHAT is the final need of our ground-floor premises, if
they are to bear the weight of the upper story; the thrust
and pressure of the supernatural life? The Saints reply,
with one voice: Fortitude, strength, staying-power! To
be 'stablished, strengthened, settled'—not etherealized,
exalted, illuminated—is St. Peter's supreme desire for
his converts. It is the sober ambition of a realist who
has known in his own person the disasters that await a
fervour based on feeling rather than will. The perfect
work of Prudence and Temperance is to make our natural
humanity 'strong in the Lord'; so establish the soul's
house on the rock, and make its walls solid, that it can
carry those strange upper works which are part of the
builder's design.

The ground floor, rising up from the natural order, is
subject to its law of consequence; all the vicissitudes
of circumstance, health, opportunity, the ebb and flow
of energy and inclination, the temperamental reaction of
the souls with whom we must live. Through these, God
reaches us, deals with us, trains us; and to the uttermost.
That living Spirit pressing so insistently on our spirits,
filling with its spaceless presence every room of the soul's
house, yet comes to us in and through natural circumstance; and makes of this circumstance, however homely,
the instrument of its purifying power. The touch of the
eternal reaches us most often through the things of sense.
We are called to endure this ceaseless divine action; not

with a sullen stoicism, but with a living grateful patience. The events by which we are thus shaped and disciplined are often as much as the natural creature can bear. God comes to the soul in His working clothes, and brings His tools with Him. We need fortitude if we are to accept with quietness the sharp blows and persistent sand-papering which bring our half-finished fitments up to the standard required by the city's plan. But it is this steady endurance, born of the humble sense that everything which happens matters, yet only matters because it mediates God, and offers a never to be repeated opportunity of improving our correspondence with God, which more and more makes the house fit to be a habitation of the Spirit. It is not a week-end cottage. It must be planned and organized for life, the whole of life, not for fine weather alone. Hence strong walls and dry cellars matter more than many balconies or interesting garden design.

The winds will blow and the floods come to the very end; overwhelming events, wild gales of feeling and impulse, will sweep round the walls. The doors will bang and windows rattle. The bitter, cold and penetrating waters of disappointment and grief will rise. But the little house will stand firm, if it is established on the solid rock of spiritual realism; not the soft easily-dug ground of spiritual sentiment. Its foundations must go down into the invisible world of prayer: something of the steadfastness of the Unchanging must underlie our human changefulness. The balance between the different parts, with their compensating thrusts and strains, must keep the walls true. If one becomes excessive, and pushes too much, the house may fall.

That the soul's self-giving prayer and work should be really costly and difficult, should call for the putting out of a definite degree of effort, should involve a certain tension and even pain—all this is surely good. The job that is done quite easily is seldom done quite well. However we conceive it—whether as pilgrimage, or growth—the spiritual life of man is never without an element of conflict. Effort and endurance must enter deeply into the process by which our mixed being is harmonized, simplified, expanded, and made fit to be the instrument of God. For those in whom there is a pronounced disharmony between natural temperament and supernatural call, the struggle may be bitter until the very end; and it is better that it should so continue, than that we should harmonize ideal and achievement on a lower level than the best possible, and so false to the city's building-law. We are not to yield an inch to the bungalow-ideal of human character. But this rightful interior tension should never threaten our spiritual equilibrium. When Fortitude begins to be coloured by strain, and action tends to become agitation, we are approaching the danger zone of the soul's life. That soul is required to be a 'fixed abode for God through the Spirit'; and for this, something of the still peace of the Eternal, 'never changing state into the contrary' must toughen its fragility, temper its restlessness. The paradox of peaceful striving runs right through the New Testament. Fortitude means the achievement, even on the natural level, of an inward stability which transcends the world of change. The small size of our premises matters little, if the walls are weather-proof and stand firm.

Such fortitude is not the virtue of the dashing soldier. It means rather the virtue of the keeper of the fortress; the inconspicuous heroism that sits tight. And in the life of the spirit there is a great deal of sitting tight; of refusing to be frightened out of it or decoyed away from it; of refusing to despair, waiting till the weather improves, till business gets brisker, day breaks, the shadows lift.

We must endure a mysterious pressure, which operates more often and more purely in darkness than in light. We cannot take up the soul's privileges and responsibilities as a householder of the Spiritual City, merely by paying one instalment and getting immediate delivery of all the goods we desire, with an insurance policy protecting us from risk; so that there is nothing to do but settle down cosily in our freshly furnished rooms. That citizenship is the beginning of a new life; a total sublimation of experience, in which all life's tensions and possibilities are raised to a higher term. More demand on prudence and initiative, keener struggle than before; a new capacity for joy, but also a new capacity for pain. It means incorporation in that Mystical Body, through which the awful saving power of God is poured out on the world: and taking our small share in filling up the measure of those sufferings by which alone redeeming work is done. The Holy City stands on a rock; but in the midst of a world of sin and pain. And the price of citizenship, as regards contact with that world, is likely to include suffering and loneliness, much misunderstanding, much self-giving with little apparent result. It may go further, and require that entire and pure act of resignation, that self-oblation even to the uttermost, which was once accomplished in Gethsemane, and remains the clue to the whole redeeming and creative life. The soul needs Fortitude, if it is to take up that great vocation.

Baron von Hügel speaks gratefully in one of his letters of 'My little old life which God has *deigned* to train by not a few trials'. It is this deeply grateful recognition of the Divine action, as specially discovered in those disciples and sufferings which teach Fortitude to the soul, and toughen it to take its share in the sacrificial action of the Body of Christ, which distinguishes from the devotee the truly awakened spirit, the living acting member of the Communion of Saints. An uncalculating surrender of our own premises to the general purpose, losing all individual preferences and reluctances in the vast outlines of God's mysterious design, is the condition of that membership: and to be able to make this willed surrender, is the most solemn dignity of the human soul. It means a sober willingness to renounce all spiritual enjoyments, in order to take up the burden of the world's wrongness; put up in our own persons with the results. All must suffer; the lesson of Christianity is what can be done with suffering, when it is met with self-oblivious courage and love.

'To him that overcometh is promised Angels' Food: and to him that is overcome, much misery,' says Thomas à Kempis. The breaking of bread, without the cup of the Passion, is only half the Eucharistic secret. We do not understand that secret till we see the Eucharist and the Cross as two aspects of one indivisible act. The communicant is merely what St. John of the Cross roughly calls a 'spiritual glutton' unless this rich mysterious action involves for him a complete and sacrificial self-giving for the saving purposes of God; unless he makes his tiny contribution to that perfect work of charity, which is the eternal act of Christ.

The supernatural food is given, the little separate life fed and enhanced, that it may be gathered, itself a lively sacrifice, into the great sacrificial movement of the Divine life. 'He that eateth dwelleth in Me, and I in him.' But the energy thus received from beyond the world, must be met by the soul's self-oblivious fortitude, its spirit of steadfast endurance, staying power. Fervour is not enough. We need the grit that puts things through in spite of apparent failure, or the shrinking horror of the flesh: that achieves its victory by way of the lonely darkness of the Garden, the more lonely and terrible darkness which fell at midday upon the Cross. Those whose courage and fidelity failed at the first withering touch of the Passion had just experienced in their own persons the solemn and touching mystery on which the Church lives still. By it their spirits were made willing; but their flesh was weak. And however great the peace and joy that welcome the soul when it elects for the spiritual life, it will not be long before it, too, experiences the fundamental need of Fortitude if it is to be faithful to the supernatural call. Its true initiation into the realities of that call, comes with the first secret stand-up fight with a temptation, desire, or attachment that truly attracts it; the first deliberate sacrificial death to sin and self. That means deep suffering, whatever form it takes: and included in it, is the temptation to abandon a job that seems beyond our feeble powers.

The soul, said Coventry Patmore, 'dies upon the Cross every time it resists interior temptation even to despair'. We must be crucified to the world, the downward pull, not once, but again and again; because the conflict between the two lives persists in us till holiness is reached. The Cross stands on the frontier between the natural and supernatural worlds. Thus the bracing of natural character is essential if we are to bear the tensions of the supernatural life. It is a stern business. It enters into conflict, it goes on being in conflict, with all in us that is turned towards the world. The principles of Christianity are absolute; they reflect Eternity. The principles of the world may be judicious, amiable, beneficent. But they are contingent: they arise from, and are adapted to a world of change. Christianity looks beyond the world's flux to God, the unchanging Reality. It seeks the increasing incarnation of His Spirit; and for that sake accepts a standard of purity, renunciation and forgiveness alien to the interests of the world. Thus, to live in the world and not of it—and this is the situation for which our house is made—requires much fortitude, a love that is loyal and courageous rather than demonstrative: 'not worn out with labours, not daunted with any difficulties.'

We are committed to a swaying battle, not an easy victory; and our worst enemies are those of our own house. Again and again our temperamental devils will be too much for us; ingrained habits, inherited tendencies, will fling us into the dungeon of impotent despair. It is with our spiritual as with our physical maladies. When we have faithfully used all rightful means of healing, a certain residuum may remain; some humiliating weakness, or chronic malformation we cannot cure, but can make an occasion of patience, courage, surrender. 'Fear none of those things thou shalt suffer.' If our first experience of the life of spirit comes with the lovely glow of victory which rewards a bit of costly self-conquest; perhaps the second, and more real experience comes when we attempt a further struggle with our unfortunate ground-floor conditions in our own strength, and fail abjectly. For then we are thrown back upon God, the only source of strength; and abruptly reminded that contempt of self is said to be the city's law. 'When I am weak, then I am strong.' The *Miserère*, the classic poem of penitence, is all about this paradoxical power of the soul which abides in its own nothingness; the abandonment as it were of all trust in its own poor individualized bit of moral energy, and the receiving instead of a mysterious participation in the Spirit of living strength.

Certainly our own preliminary effort and struggle are needed. Fortitude does not merely consist in waiting about; but in a real bracing of the will to courageous action. It is to him that overcometh, that the fruit of the Tree of Life is given. 'Will and grace rise and fall together.' Ghostly strength is like one of those funds to which the Government adds £1 for every pound subscribed voluntarily. It is the reward of really trying to do or bear something for God; not of wanting to do or bear something. As even the most impressive view from the hotel terrace tells nothing of the real secret of the mountains, which is only imparted to those who will turn their backs on comfort, take the risks; so the passive appreciation of the spiritual landscape, the agreeable reading of mystical books—fruit of the courage and love of other souls, but making no demand on ours—gives us no genuine contact with the things of God. We must put on our own boots, face the early start and long slow plod through the lower pastures, where the mountains are seldom in view—make a rule of life, and practise it in the teeth of reluctance and discouragement—if we want to share the life of the mountaineer; know the strange rapture of communion with the everlasting hills.

'No one can come to the sublime heights of the Divinity,' said the voice of the Eternal Wisdom to Suso, 'if they have not experienced the bitterness and lowliness of My humanity.' That is the soul's testing ground. It is there, under ordinary human conditions and subject to their humbling limitations, that it gets its training for the heights; purges its love of comfort, learns patience, shows its grit. There it discovers that fortitude does not mean any spectacular display of gallantry; but sticking it out in fog and storm, loneliness and disillusion—going on and on, in spite of the cuts and bruises to affection, dignity and self-esteem, never unnerved by the endless tumbles, the dull fatigue, through which it must ascend in heart and mind, accomplish the work of sacrifice and prayer. Fortitude means the courage of the lonely soldier in an isolated corner; the courage of one whose friends deserted Him in the crisis; the courage of the naked will alone with the Will of God. Manhood is incomplete till it has known the agony of spiritual isolation in a crowded world: endured with fortitude the desolation and helplessness of the soul over against surrounding mystery. According to tradition our Lord fell three times under the weight of the Cross; but rose and went on, with full knowledge that worse suffering, more bitter humiliation, lay before Him.

We see again and again in the lives of the Saints how constant and definite is the demand made on this courage and endurance; which is the natural expression of their heroic, unlimited, supernatural love. It is by way of the difficulties, sufferings and humiliations of the natural life that they cure the soft human horror of the austere side of the spiritual life, test and brace their growing spirits, make them capable of its full privileges and responsibilities. Little quarter is given to those in whom this total transformation is begun. 'His Majesty,' says the ever-valiant Teresa, 'loves a courageous soul'; and, old and very ill, struggling in the teeth of circumstance to make her last foundation at Burgos, she hears the inner voice which has been the support of all her labours, saying 'Now Teresa, be strong!' So too the angel who visited Suso in the hour of his utmost trial, did not offer him a devotional aspirin; but merely made the astringent remark 'Behave like a man!' That was Suso's immediate task; the way in which his soul was cleansed and strengthened, and brought to 'the Upper School of Perfect Self-Abandonment'.

So our survey of the ground floor of the soul's house brings us to the acceptance of this ideal of a disciplined normal humanity, deepened and organized, 'stablished, strengthened, settled' as the true basis of a spiritual life. The peaceful, temperate and balanced employment in God of those natural faculties and opportunities committed to us, choosing with self-oblivious love what helps, remembering that excess most often hinders, bearing and enduring all that the choice of His interests entails; this must bring order to our downstairs life, if the home is ever to be fit for its guest. 'Peace,' says St. Thomas Aquinas, 'is the tranquillity of order; disquiet diminishes as sanctity increases.' And if there is one characteristic which marks a genuine spiritual experience, that characteristic is surely the deep peace in which it places the soul. Thus a certain slowing down and spacing out of our ceaseless clockwork activities is a necessary condition of the deepening and enrichment of life. The spirit of Joy and the spirit of Hurry cannot live in the same house. But Joy, not Hurry, is an earnest of the Presence of God; an attribute of the creative life.

Without the steadying influences of Prudence, Temperance and Fortitude, without the wise austerity of feeling, thought and will which these require, who can hope to be quiet, and so prepare a habitation for that serene Spirit of Joy which is God? Without these, we are perpetually tormented by indecision, weakened by excesses, discouraged by failures; the trials and darkness which form part of the life of prayer defeat instead of bracing us, the very richness of experience and opportunity through which God moulds our characters, bewilders us. It is not till the ground floor is in good order that we acquire the priceless art of doing one thing at a time, and doing it with total dedication, which is the foundation of an ordered life. The sense of cleavage between the duties of Mary and Martha, and a certain uneasy effort to combine them, is responsible for much psychic untidiness, tension and weakening fuss. When the whole house is devoted to one interest, and a working harmony is established between the upper and the lower floor, each action, however homely, has the quality of prayer; since every corner and all that is done in it is informed by God and tends to God. It is the work of Prudence to discern and accept all that He proposes; because however odd it seems, it is the apt means of the soul's contact with Him. It is the work of Temperance to resist the temptation to bring in other things, crowd the soul's life with loves, labours, or devotions not truly proposed to it by God. It is the work of Fortitude to endure His moulding action with tranquillity, and maintain our steadfast correspondence with His will. In the secret world of self-conquest, in all dealings with circumstance—people, opportunities, trials, tasks—and in the most hidden experiences of the spirit, it is on this triple foundation that the soul's deep action must rest. Here is the solid basis of that truly mortified and tranquil character which can bear the stress and burden of the supernatural life.

V

WE go on to consider the upper floor of the soul's house;
the home of those faculties which point beyond our here
and now existence, which are capable of God, tend towards God, and only find their full meaning in God.
We have seen what we have to do in the way of transmuting the powers and instincts which rule the natural
life. Behaviour, Impulse, Endurance—aspects of our
living correspondence with the natural order—must all
be purified, sublimated, if the house is to become a
solid habitation of the Spirit; if its walls are to bear the
thrust of the upper floor. But the life of nature, even
in its perfection, is not enough in itself. It makes an
admirable bungalow; but the City of Mansoul is not a
bungalow town. Though it is based on the purification,
the transmutation of our common earthborn nature,
more than morality is needed for the purposes of the
spiritual life. That life requires the transfiguration in
God of the upper floor and its special powers—the stuff
of personality, the 'superior faculties of the soul' as the
old psychologists say: and this is the peculiar work of
Faith, Hope and Charity, the three 'supernatural virtues'
which imply God, tend to God, and take the soul beyond
its own resources into Him. By Faith we mean the
lifting up into God of our natural human power of
understanding the world; by Hope, the state in which
our whole mental content, our 'apperceiving mass' is

penetrated and transmuted by our confident expectation of Him; by Charity, that glowing friendship between Creator and created, which merges our will in His will. Thus all three are forms of one thirst for ultimate Being, the drive of personality towards God; and at their fullness merge into one act or state, which lifts the soul up and out beyond itself and the interests of its own small house, and beyond all merely utilitarian and this-world notions of goodness, to something more—a certain loving participation in Eternal Life.

For this, to make a home for the soul's adoring vision, confidence, and love, the house of humanity is built and kept in order. The prudence, moderation, steadfast endurance which control its domestic life, the constant death to self which they entail, are worth while, simply because they support this other life; the life that flowers in Faith, Hope and Charity, and thus incarnates something of the Eternal; the life which is in its fullest sense the life of prayer. For real prayer is simply the expression and the experience of Faith, Hope and Charity; each penetrating and enhancing the other, and merging to form in us that state of energetic and loving surrender, in which our spirits have according to their measure communion with the Spirit of God.

Thus an outlook upon the world controlled by Faith is the privilege of every house that is established in the City of God. It means the transcending of our limited anthropocentric outlook; being lifted up to a certain participation in the universal Divine outlook. Those who 'in heart and mind thither ascend and with Him continually dwell' change their angle of vision; see the world and all things in it from His point of view. A tremendous change from our ordinary way of seeing and thinking takes place then. We gaze with cleansed sight on the world we are placed in, and the life we are privileged to lead in it; perceive its richness and mystery, its utter dependence on God.

Faith—often so cheaply equated with mere belief—is something far more than this. It is the soul's watch-tower; a solitary place at the top of a steep flight of stairs. Those stairs, for some souls, have almost the character of the Way of the Cross; so humbling are the falls, so disconcerting the evidence of our human weakness, so absolute the stripping, and so complete the sacrifice which is asked as the price of the ascent. Bit by bit, all the wrappings of sensitive nature must be left behind. And even for those to whom the way lies open, and of whom this utter denudation is not asked, it is sometimes a great effort to go up. The stairs are steep; we are, or think that we are, very busy. We know that if we do go, it must be with purified sight, clear of prejudice and of distracting passions, empty of our selves; for only in emptiness of spirit, as Ruysbroeck says, can we receive that Incomprehensible Light which is 'nothing else but a fathomless gazing and seeing'. With so little leisure and so languid an inclination, it seems better to mutter a few prayers whilst we tidy the kitchen; content ourselves with the basement view of the world, and rationalize this interior laziness as humility of soul.

But if we do make the effort needed for that ascent, what a revelation! Busy on the ground floor, we never realized that we had a place like this; that our small house shot up so high into Heaven. We find ourselves, as it were, in a little room with a window on each side. There is no guarantee as to what any one soul will see out of those windows, for there is always far more to see than we can apprehend. Nor is the view on any one day equally good out of each window. Sometimes it is the homely detail in the foreground that we notice; seen now in new proportion, from a fresh point of view. Sometimes that is forgotten, and the eye is drawn to the greatness and beauty of the distant hills. Sometimes the country lies before us hard and clear as a map; at others, a delicate haze gives mystery to the landscape of faith. The light, too, is variable. Sometimes the heavenly sunshine streams in with overwhelming splendour. We are warmed, dazzled, delighted; though we see nothing distinctly, the lovely radiance brings its own assurance. Sometimes we go up, to find a grey day. The view is there, but all seems cheerless; there is no joy in our faith. This does not mean that we had better go downstairs. The upper room is more than a devotional sun-trap. Faith seeks the enlightenment of the understanding, whatever pain comes with it; and shirks no truth, however bewildering, which is shown to it by God. It means a share in the outlook of one who rejoiced in spirit, yet was sorrowful even unto death; whose rich experience embraced spiritual vision and spiritual darkness too. The variations of the weather, then, should never control our faith.

Though the landscape in which our watch-tower stands is really continuous, the two windows seem to us to look out on different and contrasting worlds. The soul can never peer round the corner, and see the point at which they meet. Moreover, the windows themselves are not always the same size. Some have a great casement opening to the north, which reveals vast expanses of sky. Others, as St. Bernard says, only have narrow slits through which the rays of the Eternal Light come in; but these may have a big bow window on the other side of the tower.

The northward view is a view of infinite spaces—a wild and solemn landscape over against us, which seems without meaning for the little lives of men—a desert country full of strange beauty, which leads the eye outward to the horizon; and shows it, at an awful distance, the peaks of great mountains hanging in the air. Here the soul looks out with adoration to the vast uncharted continent of the Divine. For some, this is the window that exercises a perpetual attraction; the view exhilarates while it daunts them, the mystery in its incomparable majesty is friendly though august. It is God Pure, the soul's country, the Transcendent World in itself, that they crave for; not the bit made over to the use of man. This it is which wakes their awe-struck and delighted adoration, nourishes their souls. The stellar radiance in which they see it, is more desirable than the sunny landscapes of earth. It lifts them beyond all conflict, all self-occupation, and fills them with a solemn joy. 'Thou *art*!' cries St. Augustine as he gazes from this window, 'and art God and Lord of all that Thou hast created; and in Thy sight stand fast the causes of the transient, and the fountains of the changeable abide unchanged!'

Even though the revelation comes seldom, for this is the outlook which is most often clouded, the souls who are possessed by this thirst for the Unchanging are content to kneel by the window, and know that the unspeakable splendour of the Eternal is there. 'Here,' says Ruysbroeck, 'our reason abides with open eyes in the darkness; that is, in an abysmal ignorance. And in this darkness, the abysmal Splendour remains covered and hid from us, for its unsearchable infinitude blinds our reason, but its simplicity and self-hood enfold and transform us.' Thus even those who have yet seen nothing from this window, should resist the temptation to veil its gaunt outline in curtains embroidered with symbolic designs. As travellers who go up to Darjeeling and wait for many days to see the majestic vision of the Himalaya at dawn, a moment will come when, if they wait long enough and look high enough, they will see the mighty summits hanging in the air; and after that, the world will never be the same to them again. 'It is far better,' says Spinoza, 'to know that God's Perfections are infinite, than to persuade ourselves that we know what those Perfections are.' It was surely for the refreshment of that vision, a renewal of that still and joyous gazing on Eternal Life, that our Lord went up alone into the mountain to pray. Strength and patience, a renewed sense of proportion, come from communion with that wide horizon, that sky of uncounted stars: a wholesome humbling sense of the contrast between our tiny house and the life it shelters, and the steadfast mystery of the heavens with their unknown worlds. 'The utmost that we know of God,' says St. Thomas, 'is nothing in respect of that which He is.'

Such an outlook on the Unchanging redeems our prayer from pettiness, discounts our worries, brings a solemn selfless peace. Everything drops away except awe, longing, and humility. 'Whom have I in heaven but thee? and there is none upon earth that I desire beside thee.' The soul stands over against the eternal reality of the Universe, and finds there a friend and not a void. *Deus meus!* My God! We have, in our creaturely weakness, a personal hold upon Infinite Reality. The Psalms are full of this exultant certitude. 'O God, thou art *my* God! early will I seek thee!' St. Augustine is ever recurring to such thoughts: isolating, gazing at, the Fact of God. Thus to dwell upon the great key-words of religion gives depth and width to human prayer; clarifies the sight with which we look out upon the sky.

We turn to the window on the other side of Faith's tower. That looks out upon our homely, natural, changeful world. It shows us human life, conditions, problems, from the angle of faith; and the mystery of the Eternal self-revealed in human ways. That too is a wonderful and inspiring sight, enlightening the understanding. Though clouds pass over that landscape, storms come, seasons change, it is yet seen to be full of God's glory. The same unchanging light and life bathes the world we see out of each window. Jungle and city, church and market-place, the most homely and the most mysterious aspects of creation, are equally known as works of the Wisdom of God.

From this window the earth with its intricate life is perceived in the light of the Incarnation; God self-disclosed in and with us, as well as God over against us. The depth and mystery of Reality, its stern yet loving action, are revealed within the limitations of history, and in the here-and-now experience of men. We pierce the disconcerting veil of appearance, and discern that Holy Creativity, making, rectifying, and drawing all things to itself. At times a lovely glint transfigures even the smallest living things. We see the kitten play in Paradise. The humble inhabitants of the hedgerows suddenly reveal their origin, their kinship with God. At other times a deeper secret, the little golden rill of Holiness welling up from beyond the world of visible life, is glimpsed by us in the most unexpected situations. Yet there is no pink glass in this window. It blurs none of the dread facts; the ever-present evil, the baffling pain, the conflict and apparent failure and inequality of life. But from the angle of Faith these are seen in proportion, as material for the self-imparting of God; and for man's self-giving to God truly tabernacled among us. Through the clatter of the world, Faith hears an insistent call to purity and sweetness; and discerns in the tangle of life the perpetual emergence of an other-worldly beauty, which has its source and end in Him alone.

Even from the ground-floor level, all persons of goodwill can realize the moral beauty and deep human pathos of the Gospels; the pattern of behaviour put before us in Christ, and again and again incarnate in the Saints. But Faith, ascending in heart and mind, sees here the Living Real self-revealed in human ways to human creatures; and in every scene and mystery of this life a natural and a super-natural quality—light cast on the meaning of our strange human experience, as the medium of God's secret moulding action, and on His way with the growing souls of men. By this 'living way' as the writer of Hebrews says, and through the veil of this humanity, we penetrate to the Holiest. It is by going upstairs and gazing out of that window that we regain poise, courage and peace when our own human experience seems too much for us; for there we see it lit by a supernatural light, and one walking through that earthly landscape in all things tempted as we are yet without sin, who humbles and convicts us on the one hand—strengthens and refreshes us on the other hand. As a great artist, taking from the natural world the form and raw material of his picture, is loyal and reverent in accepting the limits of that material, subordinating his freedom to the stuff in which he works, and only thus conveys the message of his spirit; so God here gives man a picture woven of the stuff of human history and experience, which is a full and perfect revelation of His eternal Spirit in human terms. Faith lifts us to the level at which we can see this, and more and more vividly as our eyes grow clearer: shows us the express image of the Eternal Perfect revealed in a human life, of which the various and serial action depends on an unchanging contemplation of God. Above all in the mysterious power and holiness of sacrifice, the Cross, transfiguring and lifting up the created soul—though in utmost pain, darkness and confusion—to a share in the creative work of God, it finds the one enduring link between the natural and the supernatural life.

Thus, to the eye of Faith the common life of humanity, not any abnormal or unusual experience, is material of God's redeeming action. As ordinary food and water are the stuff of the Christian sacraments, so it is in the ordinary pain and joy, tension and self-oblivion, sin and heroism of normal experience that His moulding and transfiguring work is known. The Palestinian glow which irradiates the homely mysteries of the Gospel, and gives to them the quality of eternal life, lights up for Faith the slums and suburbs, the bustle, games and industries, of the modern world. Then the joys, sorrows, choices and renunciations, the poor little efforts and tragedies, of the ground-floor life, are seen to be shot through, dignified and transfigured by the heavenly radiance, the self-oblivious heroism, of the upstairs life. Nor can we exclude from a share in this transforming glory the mystery and pathos of that animal creation from which our natural lives emerge. Faith shows us each tiny creature ringed round by the celestial light. A deep reverence for our common existence, with its struggles and faultiness, yet its solemn implications, comes over us when we realize all this; gratitude for the ceaseless tensions and opportunities through which God comes to us and we can draw a little nearer to Him—a divine economy in which the simplest and weakest are given their part and lot in the holy redemptive sacrifice of humanity, and incorporated in the Mystical Body which incarnates Eternal Life.

So in this upper room, this 'spire-top of the soul' as the mystics call it, we are offered a life of prayer so full and rich that in it we can turn to—and even combine— both the great aspects of God's self-disclosure to man. If our prayer is to be adequate to our vision, there must be a place in it for the Transcendent Mystery and the Incarnate Life; for adoration and sacrament, awe and active love. But we have not finished yet with all that the upper room has to give us. There are days when we are not drawn to either window; when it is dark outside, the stars are hidden, and the landscape loses all colour and significance. What is then left for Faith? Perhaps the best thing of all: as the best hours of human life are often those when the home is closed from the outside world, the curtains are drawn and the lamp lit.

When the curtains of Faith are drawn, we find that we are not alone in the upper room. A companion is there with us, and has always been with us; when we hardly noticed—almost took for granted—when we were gazing at the marvellous view. Now in the dimness we draw near one another. As the mystics say, it is in the Night of Faith that the soul draws nearest to God; and discovers the indwelling Power whose presence does not depend on vision and feeling, but only on faithfulness. This is the 'wondrous familiarity of the blessed Presence of God' of which they often speak. Here, as Grou teaches, is that place of prayer which can never fail us; the place where our bare, naked being has contact in its ground with the Being of God—'created intelligence with In-create Intelligence, without intervention of imagination or reason, or anything else but a very simple attention of the mind and an equally simple application of the will'. Here, where the mysterious Source of all beauty, truth and love enters and obscurely touches our spirit, the most secret and intimate experiences of religion take place. Happy in her bareness and poverty, the soul sits like the beggar maid at Cophetua's feet. She has no desire to look out of the window then. She is absorbed in that general loving attention which is the essence of contemplative prayer; an attention sometimes full of peace and joy, at others without light or emotional gladness, but always controlled by a gratitude, adoration, humble affection, which exclude all thought even of the needs of self. Such prayer, said one of the mystics, 'brings God and the soul into a little room, where they speak much of love'.

Through Faith, then, the soul, shut in its little house, can receive these three disclosures of God; and respond by its adoration, adherence, humble collaboration with Him. But not all three at once; or, as a rule, all three with equal fullness and intensity. A baby may experience the mother's breast, or from the cradle gaze up at the mother's face, or clutch for safety at the mother's dress. All three are distinct and complementary experiences of the same mother; and in the dim yet vivid baby mind, the great fact of the mother already exceeds and unites all these separate experiences. So it is with Faith's vivid yet obscure experience of God: the Transcendent Mystery, the Manifest Life, the Indwelling Guest. Ascending to the 'fine point of the spirit' the soul everywhere finds Him, since there is no place where He is not; and just because of her discovery of all that is given in secret to the depths within, can dare to stretch out towards the heights above. But she must divide her experience, if she is ever to express even the fragment that can be told of it: and even so the ultimate fact 'incomprehensible yet comprehending all' escapes her. For the Divine action exceeds, while it encloses and penetrates, all the partial apprehensions of Faith. 'What shall any man say,' cries St. Augustine, 'when he speaks of Thee?'

What then is this experience, in so far as the limited mind of man can grasp it? It is an experience of Trinity in Unity: of Eternal Father, Manifest Son and Indwelling Spirit. Yet in this experience the three are known to be one: the unmeasured Light of the Godhead is truly the

Light of our world and the Inner Light of each soul. Perhaps this approximation of theology and prayer will give the traditional language of religion fresh depth, quality, and meaning for us. 'I confess to God Almighty, the Father, Son and Holy Spirit, in the sight of the whole Company of Heaven!' How overwhelming is the meaning carried by this familiar phrase, for those who stand in the watch-tower of Faith. The self-contempt engendered by our own dingy domesticities is unmeasurably deepened and purified, when the soul thus finds itself over against the living Perfection of God.

Thus Faith, and the prayer of Faith, as it becomes more realistic, raises penitence to new levels of contrition and love; and so doing, opens the door wider to God. More than this, it operates a stern cleansing of our whole understanding of existence; taking us backwards and forwards from the surrounding mystery to the human necessity, from the vast and dimly seen supernatural life to the divinely supported natural life which trains us, and inward to the soul's own secret life, divinely supported too. Three in one, all controlled and used by God in His transcendent Majesty and freedom, all subject to a vast purpose which is far beyond our knowledge, and yet in which we share. Queer little scraps of spirit, riding with comparative ease on the bosom of Creativity, we think seldom of the mysterious realities of our situation; more seldom of that spiritual economy, of which our own growing spirits must form part.

How then do we stand in respect of our use of the watch-tower of Faith? Are we so busy on the ground floor that we take it for granted, and seldom go upstairs? It is true that those stairs are dark and steep; but if we never make the effort, never ascend to the soul's summit, we remain something less than human. We miss our most sacred privilege and source of life; and our understanding of existence, our reaction to circumstance, remain petty, earthy, unpurified. Many things that look too hard to be borne at the foot of the stairs are recognized in the watch-tower as a privilege and a joy. So the first movement of prayer should always be an ascent of that staircase, a lifting up of the heart from basement levels; and the next should be an opening of the window. The air that comes in may be sharp, but it is healthy and bracing. The stuffiness and clatter of the kitchen, all Martha's worried self-important fuss, fall away from us when we breathe that air, look out on that landscape. We are standing at the apex of our spirit; and the childish absurdity of our normal troubles and pre-occupations is made plain to us. Our understanding, usually pinned down to the here-and-now, and beset by the ceaseless succession of demands and events, is being steadied and purified by contact with the Unchanging. We are lifted above the level of sense to wide horizons; and see that sense-life in new proportion, lit by a new compassion and love. Faith simplifies our sight and pacifies our minds, by subordinating all things to the Reality of God.

Certainly it may take years for our faith thus to become truly realistic. At first, we do not understand that it is not realistic. Like beginners in physical science, we live happily among its symbols; unconscious of the hidden universe with which these symbols deal. Only as we emerge into realism do we see what regions of broadening experience, of which we did not even suspect the existence, still intervene between us and that which St. John of the Cross calls the 'divine abyss of faith'. 'God,' says De Caussade, 'is the Centre of Faith; and all His words and works are like the dark rays of a sun which to our sight is darker still.' Only those who live much in the watch-tower can grasp the reality within such words as these.

Those who do, will realize how grotesque is any alliance between spiritual self-occupation and faith: how absurd is the situation of the small creature gazing from its window at the majestic spectacle of the Universe, or watching the searching drama of the Cross, or shut in the dimness with that presence whose love and lowliness so unmeasurably exceed its own whose only thought is: How can this help *me*? We have to drop all that sort of thing, kill the reflex action of our egoistic minds, achieve a little loving self-oblivion, before we can look with purity of sight upon the Real. Faith requires of the soul an adoration of God, adherence to God, collaboration with God, pursued even to forgetfulness of self. We climb the stairs obsessed by our own difficulties, prejudices and worries, weighing the pros and cons of our little affairs; secretly hoping that some holy ointment may soothe the wounds to self-importance, or repair a complexion roughened by the friction of the world. And then we are astonished because we find ourselves 'distracted', and our eyes are not in focus for the view. But if we desire to enter into our supernatural inheritance, the deep tranquillity of Faith, coming unto God we must be completely absorbed in the fact that He is; and rewards in such ways as we can endure them—and them only—that diligently seek Him for His own sake alone.

VI

THERE is a story told of an old woman who went into a
shop and asked for a quarter of a pound of 2/- tea. The
grocer asked her what sort of tea she expected to get.
She replied that she hoped for the best, but was prepared
for the worst. This, of course, was not the virtue of
Hope.

Hope, the second of those spiritual powers in man
which tend towards God, is a completely confident
expectation; that sureness and certitude with which the
awakened soul aims at God and rests in God. It is the
source of that living peace, that zest and alertness, that
power of carrying on, which give its special colour to
the genuine Christian life. Hope brings the exalted
vision of Faith into the wear and tear of our daily life.
When we descend from the watch-tower, where we feel
that we can do all things—or rather that in us all things
can be done—and try to do the things, the first result is
usually disillusion. Unless Hope has come downstairs
with us to sweeten fortitude, permeate the content of
our minds, the last result may be apathy and
despair.

The old moralists said that Hope was the virtue which
purified the Memory and made it fit for God; and by
Memory they meant all our funded experience, that
hoarded past which we drag along with us, and which
conditions our whole outlook on life. In respect of all this,
Hope teaches us the art of wise forgetting; of dropping

the superfluous, the outgrown, the trivial. It cleanses the mind from all those half-realities which impede the total concentration of our love and will on God; and lifts up all the rest of our experience into the eternal light, saying: 'Even though I do not see the meaning, yet I know all this is conditioning my growth, purifying my spirit, taking me towards You; and nothing matters but that.'

Hope finds all life penetrated by a significance that points beyond itself, and has a trustful expectation that the ceaseless stream of events, thoughts, joys, trials—the whole stuff of experience—means something, contributes to something; and only has value because it points beyond itself to God, is an earnest of rich fields of experience awaiting the soul. Such Hope is the bright side of self-abandonment. Much so-called self-abandonment is conceived in the spirit of the 2/- tea; but that real self-abandonment to God which is the supreme expression of our human freedom, should be a delighted act of Hope. 'O God, my hope is in Thee,' does not mean, 'I have tried everything else first.' It means that the final achievement of His hidden purpose is what we really care about, and that we entirely depend on Him for the power of achieving our little bit of His plan.

Thus the pain and disappointment, the tragedy and frustration of existence, are transfigured when Hope purifies the mind. If Faith enlarges and illuminates the understanding, shows it the fields of experience that lie beyond its span, Hope integrates Faith's vision with the very texture of our common thoughts, our mental life as a whole; merging the interests of that little life in the vast interests of the Divine love and will. 'When I am in trouble, I will think upon God,' said the Psalmist; think about that mysterious and living love pressing in on human history, and here and there working through in the shimmer of holiness, the sharp glint of sacrifice. I will forget my personal discomfort, my unsteadiness and anxieties, and anchor myself there. It is true that my little boat rolls heavily on the surface of the waves, and often makes me feel very ill; but under those waves is the firm ground of Reality, the Life of God. This sense that beyond all appearance we depend utterly on the Goodness of God, and can depend on it—this is Hope. 'Thy goodness,' says Thomas à Kempis, 'never ceases to do well by me.'

Such Hope gives the spiritual life its staying power. It is the necessary condition of keeping things going and getting things done. The struggles to which the ground floor of human nature commits us will never be maintained, unless that living spirit presides upstairs. As life goes on, nothing but Hope, its supernatural zest and adventurous temper, will preserve us from the insidious tendency to settle down into making religious pot-boilers; reproducing our old designs, instead of moving on to the things that are before. It is the very soul of the life of prayer; whether that prayer be poured out for the world's betterment, for the many shortcomings of our own premises and performances, or directed beyond all thought of self and world to God its Home: for it is the property of Hope, says St. Thomas, 'to make us tend to God, both as a good to be finally attained, and as a helper strong to assist'.

Thus Hope is supremely the virtue of the incomplete; of the creature stretching out in love and prayer to the complete Reality of God, the final object of Hope. In this double, trustful tendency to Him, as at once our Companion and our Goal, Faith achieves its perfect work. God whose vast purposes may be veiled from us, but whose personal, moulding, cherishing action, whose urgent and demanding Spirit, is felt at work within our little homes.

Such Hope inspires and upholds the prudence, temperance and fortitude required of us in our dealings with life and with the peculiarities of our own basement. Even its many falls are like the falls of eager children. They are dreadful at the moment, and often make us bruised and muddy. But we pick ourselves up and go on; forgetting that which is behind, reaching forward to that which is before, because there is something more at stake than 'Safety first'.

Even on the psychological level, we all experience the creative power of Hope. Our minds are so made that convinced assurance, trustful expectation, always tends to realize itself. It concentrates energy on the matter in hand, creates a favourable psychic atmosphere, encourages the will to flow undivided along the path leading to fulfilment, and sets going the appropriate mechanisms. Hence those who ask with confidence are likely to receive, and those who seek to find. Whether in that corporate life of souls which we call history; in the personal work of costly transformation to which each separate soul is committed; or in that secret and most sacred flight to God, in which the human spirit achieves its goal, Hope is the living spirit of transcendence, the pathfinder of life.

In history we see Hope as the spiritual preparation of the future; and a preparation which is left entirely in our hands. It is the way in which the corporate soul of man stretches out to lay hold upon the gifts of God. Did we look with more loving attention at God's work in history, it would help us to discern His secret workings in the soul. History, even that which we call secular history, always shows us Hope going before, to make plain the path along which the creative purpose shall move. It is the growing point of life. Social justice, education, child welfare, women's freedom—all these were hoped for long before they were achieved. And now, looking towards the future, it is the solemn duty of every awakened spirit to enlarge, deepen and enrich this hope for mankind. Every movement of pessimism is a betrayal of the purposes of God; a short-circuiting of the spiritual energy that flows from Him through living souls. The web of life is infinitely sensitive to the morbid activity of each of its cells. There can hardly be a more lethal weapon than the mind of a nation filled with the thought that war must come, or that society is running downhill; and some responsibility for this corporate mind rests upon every citizen. Thought is a great and sacred force given to us by God; our share in the life that lies behind appearance. It is a creative force when filled with Hope; a destructive force when it concentrates on the ground floor and its often deplorable state, and calls this 'facing reality'. Hence the building up of a public opinion full of Hope, because it tends with confidence to God and the things of God, is a spiritual duty laid upon all Christians; who are bound to believe in the continuous incarnation of His Spirit in human life, and to make plain the paths along which that Spirit can move. We do nothing for the Kingdom by going into the garden to eat political or ecclesiastical worms.

The whole of Christian history really turns upon the power of human hope: this absolute hold upon the reality of God, His supernatural energy and freedom, with the corresponding conviction that He does and will act within the human arena, intervene to save. 'I am not a God afar off: I am thy Maker and friend'—a Maker who has not finished His work, but is making us all the time, whose capacity for loving action is inexhaustible. The psychological landscape in which the greatest event in man's spiritual history was prepared, was coloured by Expectation, Hope. Christ was born among those who waited for the consolation of Israel; who were sure, in spite of baffling appearance, that the purpose of God would be fulfilled. The Blessed Virgin, standing at the budding-point of Christian history, meets her strange destiny with selfless confidence. The same necessary condition runs through the Gospels. Those are healed that come hopefully; their confident expectation is always approved. We are to expect that God will give us good gifts, answer our prayers, provide for our necessities. This note recurs perpetually in all our Lord's teaching. If we ask we get, if we seek we find, if we knock hopefully on the door it will open. The unlimited world of eternal life is here on the threshold with its riches; it is for us to stretch out to it with confidence. If we are not more spiritually effective, it is because of our low level of desire, our lack of initiative, of courageous expectation. The Spirit of God works in and with the faithful, hopeful will that expects, and waits upon, the supernatural response. The lessons of psychology are lifted up, and shown to us as shadows cast by the laws of the spiritual world.

In His own prayer, our Lord rejoices because all happens and must happen according to the mind of God; even though that fulfilment is reached by paths which cut across our human notions of success. In the events of Holy Week He teaches by demonstration the lesson of an unconquerable Hope; the anchoring of the soul's trust, beyond all appearance, in the infinite Life of God. From the poor little triumph of Palm Sunday, through the gathering cloud of foreboding, to the stress and agony of Gethsemane and Calvary—with an ever-increasing sense of isolation, forsakenness and darkness, culminating in the utter helplessness and ignominy of the Cross—the soul of Christ moves with a steadiness transcending human agony: sure that in spite of appearances the Will of God is holy, and that along these dark paths, by utmost sacrifice and apparent failure, the purposes of His Love must prevail. That supernatural Hope transfigured even the awful moment of dereliction, when He felt himself to be abandoned by God, and tasted the horrors of spiritual death. It was through this darkness that He rose to the heights of self-abandoned trust. 'Father, into Thy hands I commend my spirit'—the evening prayer of every Jewish child—'I do not ask, know, or guess, what is going to happen; Thou art my Hope!'

'Christ,' said the poet Péguy, 'was the Man of Hope.' He showed it in a heavenly splendour only possible to those whose lives are lost in God. Here we leave human fortitude and courage, the mere Stoic power of sticking it out, far behind; are caught in the mighty current which sets from the natural to the supernatural life, and learn that the very anguish of the soul on these frontiers of experience is an earnest that the expectation of the creature will be fulfilled. Devout persons speak much of Easter Hope; but it is surely the Good Friday hope, with its lesson of self-oblivious confidence in life's blackest moments, that speaks most clearly to the needs of men. It is then that the Church, with true instinct, exclaims, '*Agios ischyros! Agios athanatos!*' By that contemplation we are lifted from all petty preoccupation with our own reasons for despondency, taught to look on wide horizons, depersonalize our prayer; confident that in suffering and apparent failure we contribute to the mysterious purposes of the God we love.

We come down from this tremendous revelation, to look at something a little nearer to our average level, and consider the work of Hope in the cleansing and re-ordering of our own soul's life. We remember how Dante places at the beginning of the *Purgatorio* a wonderful picture of the ship of souls, driven towards the purifying

mountain by the great wings of the Angel of Hope.
There they are, with all their human imperfections, stains
and limitations; and with their faces set towards the infinite possibilities, the unspeakable perfections of God.
They know that much suffering and difficult purification
must be the path along which they will reach Him;
but Hope of God, thirst for God, overrules all fear of
pain. As the ship comes to shore, they fling themselves
on the land crying: 'Who will show us the way to the
cleansing mount?' There is no reluctance to face the
penalty of conduct, the working of that law of consequence which burns out the very root of man's self-love.
They look beyond all that to God, the soul's *Patria*,
towards which they tend in hope.

We know, in our lucid moments, that we too are
committed to such a painful re-ordering of our love;
some cleansing discipline must set our muddled lives
in order, deal with the stains and excesses we have
accumulated during our tenancy, if the creature is to be
made fit for God its Home. When the radiance of the
Holy shines on our defenceless souls, we shall know ourselves for what we are. 'Then said I, Woe is me! . . . for
mine eyes have seen the King, the Lord of Hosts.' Then
the measure of our Faith, Hope and Charity will be the
gladness with which we welcome the humiliations which
must break our foolish pride, the lessons of patience that
must curb our childish anger, the deprivations that will
turn our possessive instincts from unreal to real objectives.
But if this be so, how artificial, how deficient in realistic
Hope, is that notion of God's action on and in our
spirits, which refers to an unknown future the opportunity
of purgation. The cleansing touch is already completely
present in all the ups and downs, the trials, sacrifices,
humiliations of our personal and professional life; in all
those inequalities of health, affection, opportunity, which

mortify self-will and self-esteem. It is the business of Hope, tending here and now to God, to recognize within these baffling accidents the operations of Creative Love, and its own duty of collaboration; looking fairly and squarely at all that needs to be done to fit the soul for its destiny, and then starting the work in perfect confidence that the energy of God is with us from the moment that we really take the scrubbing-brush into our hands.

The house of the soul is properly furnished; the cleaning materials are all there. The languors and difficulties of ill-health, the friction of uncongenial temperaments, the hard rubs of circumstance, can all leave us cleaner than before. As there is nothing more destructive of serenity than unwilling endurance of a spring-clean; so there is nothing more exhilarating than the same process when we do some of the work ourselves. If our own hands carry the cherished bundle of rubbish to the dustbin, if we acquiesce in the fact that the far too comfortable sofa does crowd up our room too much, and has got to go; if we put zest and hope into the struggle to efface those black marks from walls that were meant to be white—then even the most painful effort is transformed by the knowledge that we are working to make our house what it is meant to be and can be: a habitation fit for the Spirit now. We are creatures for whom the Beauty of Holiness is a possibility; in so far as we place our confidence in the perpetual operations of that Spirit which 'has marvellously made our human nature, and still more marvellously remakes it' and accept with love and courage the method by which the work is done—centring our sense of reality there, and letting all the rest drop away.

For the true basis of the soul's hope of God is God's hope for the soul. His confident intention precedes and inspires ours, and gives all its significance to our life. God's hope for souls often seems to us to be thwarted; but it begins again in its power and freshness with every baby born into the world. Each represents a hope of God; a possibility of holiness, fullness of life. He has made us for Himself; but the fulfilment of that hope is partly in our own hands. It requires our generous and courageous response to the secret Divine incentive, our peaceful acceptance of purification, our active charity; the full and dedicated use of all the resources of the upper floor. Our own reluctance, cowardice, want of hope, keep us back. 'The weakest of sinners,' said Péguy, 'can either frustrate or crown a hope of God.' When we think of this aspect of our freedom, of our ever-growing mobile, never-finished lives—that there is one fragment of the Eternal purpose which no one else can fulfil, one place in the world where we and none other are meant to transmit God's life and love, and so fulfil His Hope —then even in our timid souls there is born a faint desire to give ourselves without reserve to His purpose, whatever the cost.

There is work which God requires to be done by each one of us, and which no one else can do. Therefore our business is to get down to it, checking the instinctive recoil to the inferiority-complex, the easy resort to 'I'm not up to it: there must be some mistake'; in sure and certain hope that if we get the job, we shall get the authority it requires. 'He gave power and authority to the twelve,' says the Gospel; not merely to the most spiritual and enlightened. It does not appear that the majority were very spiritual or very enlightened; but they were free from the introspective weakness which perpetually strokes its own imperfections, and makes of them a reason for its deprecating reluctance to serve. The Twelve must have felt very odd when they were sent out alone to teach and heal; but they went with Hope, and they came back with Joy. And the same thing has ever been true of the Saints, and of countless souls far below the level of the Saints, who have accepted in the spirit of Hope an infinite variety of jobs. 'I said to God that it was His business I was about, and after that I found it very well performed,' said Brother Lawrence, when called from contemplation to buy wine for his convent—a business for which he knew that he had no capacity.

Hope of that quality is the source of the gay courage with which the real lover of God faces the apparently impossible or the unknown: and we observe that it is not merely an easy and comfortable optimism. It means acting upon our assurance, taking risks for it; entering upon a path of which we do not see the end. It means 'Go forward'; not 'Wait and see', or 'Safety first'. Forgetting the things which are behind, this hope reaches forth with confidence unto the things which are before; stripping off all that impedes it, refusing to be clogged by old fears and prejudices, moribund ideas. It believes in the God of the future, as well as the God of the past. It knows how to combine a living suppleness and freedom with an utter self-abandonment, a humble self-knowledge with a vigorous initiative. 'What is my hope? Even Thou, O God! Though I lost my temper yesterday, you *can* use me to help a soul to-day.'

'The self-satisfaction of the finite,' says Bernard Bosanquet, 'is the portal where Hope vanishes.' But once the great principle of doing nothing in our own strength is grasped, we shall find with surprise that our performance is not much affected by our own dreadful mediocrity. Something else, a stronger, richer, steadier life, supports, controls and acts through us. The guest for whom we have made room is running the house. Hope means being prepared for this, and trusting it, when we are definitely given a job, placed in a situation, which we feel to be beyond our powers; and which, for that very reason, contributes to the soul's growth by throwing it back upon God.

So Hope must preside over the soul's cleansing and re-ordering of its premises, and the work it has to do. But our supernatural Hope has a dignity and a sanction far beyond these here-and-now objectives; and asks of the creature a courage and sacrifice commensurate with its transcendental goal. We find its true image in that natural order, where the Saints have so often followed their model in looking for the supernatural lessons of God: in the autumn migrants, starting on their immense journey along the invisible pathways of the air, towards a summer home which they cannot see, yet which draws them by an irresistible power. Migration is not an easy or a pleasant thing for a tiny bird to face. It must turn deliberately from solid land, from food, shelter, a certain measure of security, and fly across an ocean unfriendly to its life, destitute of everything it needs. We make much of the heroism and endurance of our airmen and explorers. Perhaps some day men will rival the adventurous hope of the willow wren and the chiff-chaff; an ounce and a half of living courage, launching out with amazing confidence to a prospect of storms, hardship, exhaustion—perhaps starvation and death. Careful minds would hardly think the risk was worth taking. But the tiny bird, before conditions force it—not driven by fear, but drawn by Hope—commits itself with perfect confidence to that infinite ocean of air; where all familiar landmarks will vanish, and if its strength fails it must be lost. And the bird's hope is justified. There *is* summer at the other end of the perilous journey. The scrap of valiant life obeys a true instinct, when it launches itself on the air. It is urged from within towards a goal it

135

can attain; and may reckon the suffering of the moment not worthy to be compared to the glory that shall be revealed.

Our Lord found great significance in the life of birds; in their freedom, their self-abandoned trust, their release from mere carefulness. He held them precious to God, and patterns for the faith and hope of man. I sometimes think that the divine gift of Hope—that confident tendency of the soul, that trust in the invisible, and in a real goal, a Country, truly awaiting us—poured into man by God to give meaning and buoyancy to his life: all this was first, as it were, tried out in the birds. Long ages before we appeared, the clouds of tiny migrants swept over the face of this planet. Incarnate scraps of hope, courage, determination, they were ready at a given moment to leave all and follow the inward voice; obeying the instinct that called them in the teeth of peril and difficulty, giving themselves trustfully to the supporting air.

Nor does this exhaust their likeness to the soul. If we ask why the bird is so utterly at home—what is the cause of this confidence, this buoyancy, this easy, steady flight—science replies that it is itself partly a creature of air. Its very bones are so made, that the air penetrates and informs them. It is lifted from within, as well as supported from without; the invisible Kingdom to which it gives itself is inseparably a part of its own life. Even so are we both penetrated and supported by an ocean of Love and Life, an infinite yet indwelling Reality experienced though unseen: 'God in Himself as He is everywhere and at all times,' as St. Thomas has it. 'And now what is my hope? surely my hope is in Thee'— as the bird in the air, so we in the Being of God. As the bird, we are called to another country, a *Patria*. The courage which can face long effort, vast and lonely distances, apparent emptiness, may be the testing condition of our flight. Yet the loneliness and emptiness are only apparent: for in Him we live and move and have our being, even while to Him we tend. He inspires and supports the adventure of which He is the goal. For Hope is Love, tending to God at all costs; bearing all things, believing all things, enduring all things, because sure that He has made us for Himself, and our hearts shall find their rest in Him alone.

VII

WE have inspected both floors of the soul's house; stood in its watch tower, and studied its domestic arrangements—the disadvantages and possibilities of the double situation in which we are placed. Yet there still seems something lacking; something which must fill the whole house from basement to attic and bind in one both levels of life, if its upkeep is to be worth while, if it is to be anything more than a model dwelling without the atmosphere of a home. What is it that is wanting? Charity; the living Spirit of Creative Love. To be a home, a dwelling-place in time for that Spirit, the house has been swept and garnished, the best loved bits of rubbish have been sacrificed, the windows have been cleaned, the table set. It is not intended to be a show-place, but a real 'habitation of God through the Spirit'; and the name of the Spirit is Charity. If Faith opened the eyes of the understanding on that threefold vision in which we see that only God is fully real; and if Hope so purified the mind's content that all dropped away but its trustful tendency to that unchanging Reality; then Charity transforms in God the very mainspring of character, the active will, and thus completes the spiritualization of man.

So Charity, when it enters the soul's house, swallows up and irradiates its Faith and Hope. 'God *is* Charity,' says St. John, 'who dwells in Charity dwells in God'—

a saying which might deliver us from much anthropomorphic pietism, did we realize its depth and sweep. It means that the Spirit of Creative Love is the very character of the Infinite God. There is no difference between saying God 'comes' to the soul in Himself, or 'sends' His love; for in that love we receive, in a way that we can bear, the impact of the ever-present Divine life upon the creature it has made. When we depart from that love we depart from Reality; leave the vivid world of spiritual fact, and enter the museum-like atmosphere of theology, full of stuffed birds that once were living bits of Faith and Hope. For the Charity of God is, as it were, the air that bathes the city, the sun that lights it, the heat that warms it; and, as experienced in each little house, by each separate soul, there is in it something of all these. If a spark from that fire burns on the hearth of personality, the soul has become to that extent a partaker of the Divine nature. She shares in the very life of the Saints; receives and distributes something of that radiant warmth which fills the whole spiritual universe, the 'Love that makes all things fair'. 'We have,' says St. Teresa, 'the Sun in our house': that Sun which is not the soul's self, but is the soul's life. Like central heating, its influence is felt everywhere, upstairs and downstairs too; distributing an equable fostering warmth to every corner, conditioning our growth into fullness of personality.

Charity, then, means something which far exceeds altruism. It is the human spirit's share of the Divine life: there is, indeed, no other way in which it can share that life. 'Who dwells in charity dwells in God'; is united to God; partakes of the creative point of view. We are looking with awe at the approach made by the human soul to the burning heart of Reality—an approach only made possible by the prevenient action of God— and, turning to our own narrow hearts, our feverish and claimful desires, unreal objectives, and fluctuating love, we ask: Can these things be? In our own strength, of course, they could not be; but they can be, because the initiative lies with the Divine life. As theology says: 'We love Him because He first loved us.' Before the stellar universe, before the first mysterious beginnings of creation, the fire of Charity was already lighted. Creation is an act of love; love, as Julian of Norwich was taught in her vision, is its 'meaning'—however much that meaning has been overlaid and distorted by the sins and confusions of life. No religious system is worth accepting or imparting that is not in harmony with this mysterious truth: for life, the 'more abundant life' of the Eternal World which is offered by God to men, can only be measured in terms of love.

'*O luce eterna piena d'amore!*' cries Dante, caught for one dazzling moment to a vision of the Real. Unless our tendency to God brings us ever nearer the point at which we see the world and all things in it in this generous transfiguring light, it is not a reality; nor is any spiritual experience valid, which fails to introduce us into that Ocean of Creative Love. 'How could those books have taught me Charity?' said St. Augustine, as he turned from the alluring mysticism of the Neoplatonists, with its tremendous appeal to his speculative intellect, and capitulated to the Cross. That was the final question for him; and still must be so, for all genuine seekers after Reality. It marks the boundary between philosophy and religion, between the objectives of the visionary and the saint. 'Without the exercise of love,' says Ruysbroeck, 'we can never possess God; and whosoever thinks or feels otherwise is deceived.'

Charity is no easy emotion. It does not merely consist in yielding to the unspeakable attraction of God. We are often terrified and always shamed, when we see what its achievement involved for the Saints; what steady endurance of darkness, what suffering and courage, are the price of their love, joy and peace. The fire of Charity, lit in the soul, needs careful tending. The first tiny flame must not be allowed to die down for lack of fuel; and we may have to feed it with things we should prefer to keep for ourselves. It will only be developed and kept burning in a life informed by prayer —faithful, steady, mortified, self-oblivious prayer, the humble aspiration of the spirit to its Source: indeed, the very object of prayer is to increase and maintain Charity, the loving friendship of the soul with God.

All other aspects of the inner life are subsidiary to this: and only of value in so far as they contribute to it. For the prayer of Charity introduces us into the very atmosphere and presence of God, that secret chamber of the soul where He dwells; and shows us, obscurely but intensely, God as the one object of this soul's love and longing, and all struggles and sacrifices made in His interests as forms of joy. It lifts the heavy cloud of self-occupation from our spirits, transforms the mental and moral problems that torture us; they all look different in the light of that fire. 'Love,' says Thomas à Kempis, 'sees causes of fear and feareth not; but as a quick brand or sparkle of fire flameth ever upward.' And it is this constant desirous aspiration of the soul towards the Beloved Perfection, with its utter forgetfulness of personal dreads and risks, which delivers it from evil. 'Adam sinned when he fell from contemplation'—and the essence of contemplation is the soul's loving attention to God. 'Were we always simple,' says Ruysbroeck, 'and could we always contemplate with the same recollection, we should always have that same experience, which is our proper resting-place.'

Within the prayer of Charity, too, we catch a glimpse

of our own small life in the light of God, and of our own soul's house as it is meant to be—a habitation of the Creative Love. It is a bracing and a humbling vision. We see our vocation then, however prosaic, as a form of Charity; simply a call to express the creative love infused into us, in this or that way. For Charity introduces the soul into a vast organism, built of all striving, loving spirits; an organism which is destined to be possessed and used by God, for creative and redemptive work within the world.

Hence the only active works worth doing or worth having, are ultimately found to be those that proceed from Charity: that are the work of a soul adhering to God and acting as His tool. This gives them what painters call 'quality'. We know how the Dutch artists could give quality to a heap of vegetables, or a child's toy. If the quality of charity is in our work, that work, however modest, will suffice. If not, all its apparent devotedness, efficiency and success will merely give out the correct but unmusical noise of the gong, or the tinkle of the bright and busy cymbal. Works of mercy done by the Saints come out, as it were almost of themselves, from a soul so utterly merged in the Love of God that He acts through it. Thus they have an effect quite out of proportion to their apparent scope. A real act of Charity is the exact opposite of an act of philanthropy. It is done wholly to, for and in God; for His sake, as a contribution to His purpose, because we see the situation from His point of view. It is born of the First, not the Second Commandment: of supernatural, not of natural, love. So too all religious acts and sacrifices—more, all sacred objects, symbols and devotions, even to the loftiest degrees of mental prayer—are only of spiritual worth if soaked in Charity and used with Charity: with a loving tendency of the naked will through them to God.

'Unless,' says Maritain, 'we direct very purely to *God alone* our desire of contemplation itself and its joys, which St. Bernard called "the paradise of interior delights", we shall not truly advance in the way of the Spirit.'

All the exercises of the devotional life fall under this law. The use of the Crucifix, meditation on Christ's Life and Passion, are found to be of value to the soul because they convey love and evoke love; and so feed the fire at the heart of personality. The disciplines and renunciations which give order and beauty to the soul's house are only fruitful when undertaken for the sake of Charity. The house is meant to radiate that; our business is to take away everything which interferes. This is the principle which gives all valid asceticism its meaning and worth. So the spirit of poverty, deliberately loosening its clutch on possessions; the spirit of chastity, calling in all vagrant, immoderate and distracting desires; the spirit of obedience, subduing its will to the over-ruling Divine Will, give health, strength and order to the love that is intended to find its goal in God: but only impoverish or sterilize the soul that is seeking for self-fulfilment by these paths. 'Charity,' says Augustine Baker, 'lives and grows according to the measure that self-love is abated, *and no further.*' We have reached the 'short point' as the lawyers say; the one thing needful, the all-sufficing rule by which the house is to be run. And we find it to be identical with the law of the city: 'Love of God even to contempt of self.'

Thus in the last resort Christian perfection, in fact the whole course of the spiritual life, is found to be the same thing as Charity—the loving union of the human spirit with the Eternal Spirit of God. Nothing but this love will drive it to the heroic struggles, self-stripping and purifications, maintain it through the long slow climb with many humbling falls, whereby it is remade in the image of the Absolute Love. The soul that plays for safety, even spiritual safety, never becomes perfect. 'Real Charity,' says St. John of the Cross, 'is not shown merely by tender feelings, but by a strength, courage and endurance unknown to other souls.' The true lover, wholly given to God and His interests, is released from all carefulness about his own interests, safety and comfort. Thus not Faith and Hope alone, but Prudence, Temperance and Fortitude too, are found in the last resort to be swallowed up in Charity.

This, then, is the first point of Charity; that pure thirst for God and complete self-giving to God—that return movement of the soul to its origin—which makes man a spiritual creature, and is the very substance of his eternal life. We go on to the second point. St. Thomas says, 'Charity includes not only love of God, but also a certain friendship with Him. It is a sign of greater love if a man devotes himself to others for his Friend's sake, than if he be willing only to serve his Friend.' That opens up another aspect of the life of Charity, and links the First with the Second Commandment—love of God Pure, and love of His creation for His sake. Adoring love alone is not enough. Charity requires us, beyond this, to place our neighbours' rights and needs on an equality with our own; because the generous love of God is poured out upon the whole world, and our love too must be perfect, complete, as that of our Father and Origin is perfect, complete.

The Cross is the supreme symbol of that double movement of Charity; the pouring forth of self-oblivious love, up towards God, outwards towards men, and surely downwards too, to all the smaller children of God. Here we are confronted by a Charity as rich, wide and deep as Creation, entirely self-giving and entirely undemanding, which loves God first, its fellows next, itself not at all;

the consummation of a life in which prayer and work, teaching and healing, joy and suffering, were simply the different strings of an instrument on which was played the only music of the Love of God. And in those Saints who approach their model most nearly, as did St. Francis, this widespreading love is the very substance of perfection, and ultimate source of their life-giving power. They are complete in their self-giving, like God. 'Because,' says Ruysbroeck, 'the living fountain of the Holy Spirit, which is their wealth, can never be spent,' they are become distributors of His creative and redeeming energy. Their passionate identification with His interests flows out in an endless variety of expression to share His love and care for other men: and it is this, more than any moral correctness, any exemption from special faults or failings, which is the earnest of their supernatural life.

So the soul's secret holy love for the One, its adoring contemplation, will flow out if it be genuine on waves of generous compassion to the Many; and especially to those whom an exact standard of merit might find unworthy of pity and care. 'To love the unlovely into lovableness' has been called the perfect work of Charity; for here we apply the Divine method to those bits of His creation that most need it: share His redeeming work.

Faith may release the mind from the tyranny of the here-and-now, and Hope may seem to concentrate the whole drive of our being upon the Reality of God. Only Charity can thus weave together both worlds, both levels of the soul's life; and, making our love of God and of His creatures one, provides a habitation, a gathering point for the Creative Love, and opens a channel through which it can be applied to each detail of His unfinished world. Thus it is, as the mystics say, that Charity makes God and the soul 'one thing'. Some of the difficulties surrounding the life of prayer, and particularly of intercession, might vanish, did we understand it as an application to particular cases of the boundless Charity of God; an application which is effected by means of our will and love.

Science sees the universe in natural regard, as a cosmic cloud of infinitely tenuous matter filling all space; and the stars as special condensations of that universal substance, able to radiate with peculiar intensity the energy we know as light—an energy which is equally present throughout space, though there unseen. An apt parable of that supernatural universe in which we live and have our being; truly continuous too, and delicately luminous with the Love of God. Within it we may think of each separate soul as a special condensation of spiritual life; able to receive and give again that energetic Charity which is poured out on all creation from the Heart of God. For each soul the final question must be; how much Charity can you receive and transmit? The Saints glow like living suns. With every aspiration towards God, the ardour of their charity increases. Its radiance penetrates to every corner of creation. It warms and vivifies the chillier worlds, which equally depend on their share in this generous and life-giving life: this one mighty movement of the Divine generosity, running right through the spiritual world, and using as its agents the loving and surrendered souls of men.

Beyond time, God loves and gives, in the changeless perfection of His Charity; and the terms on which His creatures receive, is that they should give again, heedless of self-interest and personal considerations. Thus all prayers, all sufferings, all deeds from the loftiest to the most homely, given in Charity to the purposes of God, become charged with His energy of life and avail for the perfecting of the world. In this universal sense, Charity puts us in line with all the noblest aspects of Creation— the generous outpouring of sunshine, the uncalculating fertility of the earth, the great life-giving mantle of air; all those undemanding gifts which condition our existence, and are reflected fragments of that unlimited self-giving which is the fundamental character of God.

The New Testament is full of reminders of the transcendent worth, the life-giving quality, of this generous unlimited love: the love that pours out the precious ointment, and then breaks the vase and gives that too; that throws in the second mite after the first; that sets aside as equally irrelevant personal desires, personal failings, and personal achievements. The Charity willing to feed the sheep and lambs, and go on and on chopping the turnips and tending the fold, for the sake of the Beloved: adoration and penitence blossoming in homely service. Not every one who says, 'Lord, Lord!' in accents of devotion enters the supernatural world of Charity; but only those self-given for love's sake to the purposes of the Eternal Will. Even when that Will must be carried through by means of dreary, exacting, and unrewarding labour; even where it means unlimited sacrifice for apparently unworthy ends—complete collaboration with the Divine redemptive work.

The House of the Soul, then, must be an open house for all who are sent to it; all for whom there are things to be done; all who are proposed to its fostering care. Its welcome must be as wide as that Poverty which, empty of itself, has room for all. Upstairs and downstairs, in work and in prayer, it must wholly serve the creative purpose; mortifying the desire of devotional sweetness, ignoring the claims of spiritual comfort, and bringing all the needs of the city, and of the vast desolate world beyond the city, within the area of its widespreading love. There must be room for more than two chairs on the hearthrug. The Love of God is a large generosity, not a number of intense individual love affairs; and this is the love which the living soul is called to pour out on the world. Only when it is wholly made over to His creative, saving and restoring purpose, when all that it does is done in the power of supernatural Charity, is the house indeed a habitation of the Spirit, and doing the work for which it was made. This is that union with God to which the mystics look; a union that is not con-summated in feeling, but in will and work.

The Parable of the Talents, into which we so easily read a utilitarian meaning hardly accordant with the mind of Christ, seems rather designed to enforce the lesson of the soul's responsibility in respect of this mysteri-ous gift of Charity; its share of the riches of God. Those riches are given into its care, that they may be increased and made fruitful. We are not to wrap up our bit of love, in case it might be lost or damaged; dig a hole in the soul's garden and hide it away. We are to deal with it in the world, with prudence and courage; risk it, put it out. Those who venture their Charity down in the rough and tumble of existence, submit it to the alchemy of thought, work with it boldly, and thus in-crease the living wealth of God—these are approved. The victims of a miserly, timid and unfruitful spirituality are utterly condemned. At the end of the story, it is to those who have most, that more is given: for these alone are able to receive the riches of the Kingdom of God.

'When the evening of this life comes,' says St. John of the Cross, 'you will be judged on love.' The only question asked about the soul's use of its two-storied house and the gifts that were made to it, will be: 'Have you loved well?' All else will be resumed in this; all thoughts, beliefs, desires, struggles and achievements, all the complex activities of the upper and the lower floor. For Faith is nothing unless it be the obscure vision of a loved Reality; and Hope is nothing, unless it be the confidence of perfect love. So too with all the persons, events, opportunities, conflicts and choices proposed for the soul's purification and growth. Was everything that was done, done for love's sake? Were all the doors opened, that the warmth of Charity might fill the whole house; the windows cleaned, that they might more and more radiate from within its mysterious divine light? Is the separate life of the house more and more merged in the mighty current of the city's life? Is it more and more adapted to the city's sacred purpose—the saving radiation of the Perfect within an imperfect world? For this is Charity; the immense expansion of personality effected by the love of God, weaving together the natural and the supernatural powers of the soul, and filling them with its abundant life. Overflowing the barriers of preference, passing through all contrary appearance, it mediates the Divine pity and generosity to every mesh and corner of creation; and rests at last in God, Who is the life and love of every soul.